THE RIVALS

SHERIDAN

The Rivals

edited with introduction and notes by

C. J. L. PRICE

Professor of English Language and Literature
University College of Swansea

OXFORD UNIVERSITY PRESS

Oxford University Press, Walton Street, Oxford OX2 6DP

OXFORD NEW YORK TORONTO
DELHI BOMBAY CALCUTTA MADRAS KARACHI
PETALING JAYA SINGAPORE HONG KONG TOKYO
NAIROBI DAR ES SALAAM CAPE TOWN
MELBOURNE AUCKLAND

and associated companies in
BERLIN IBADAN

Oxford is a trade mark of Oxford University Press

Introduction and notes © Oxford University Press 1968

FIRST PUBLISHED 1968
REPRINTED 1972, 1973, 1975, 1978, 1981,
1982, 1985, 1988, 1990, 1992

Printed in Hong Kong

CONTENTS

INTRODUCTION

In the second half of the eighteenth century Bath was a famous centre of fashionable life. Noblemen and their wives, squires and their ladies, sharpers, widows, painters and musicians, gathered at the spa to drink the waters, bathe in the King's bath, gossip, dance, and attend the theatre.

Among those attracted there in September 1770 was Thomas Sheridan, who hoped to institute a school of elocution. He believed that training in the articulation of ideas would do much to improve men involved in the public life of England, and managed to find a few young noblemen as his pupils. Not enough came forward to make the venture profitable so to make a living he returned to Dublin and to his old profession of acting.

His children remained in Bath for two years, and his younger son (Richard Brinsley Sheridan) later described the period as one in which he 'danced with all the women at Bath, wrote sonnets and verses in praise of some, satires and lampoons upon others, and in a very short time became the established wit and fashion of the place'. No better centre could have been found for a social education. Besides, Bath was very much in the literary news of the day for, in 1771, two of the major successes, Tobias Smollett's novel, *The Expedition of Humphry Clinker*, and Samuel Foote's play, *The Maid of Bath*, satirized life at the spa.

Foote's 'maid' was Elizabeth Linley, one of the Bath friends of the Sheridan children and a sixteen-year-old singer with a beautiful face and a heavenly voice. Her profession left her open to unwelcome advances from older men, so she decided to run away from home and asked Richard Brinsley Sheridan to accompany her as her cavalier. They crossed to France and reached Lille before her father caught up with them and persuaded her to go back to Bath. Sheridan also returned to England

and fought two fierce duels with Thomas Mathews, the man who was the immediate cause of Elizabeth Linley's flight. In the second of them Sheridan was wounded and thought to be dying. He recovered in due course, and was sent to a tutor at Waltham Abbey to prepare himself for the legal profession. Six months later, he and Elizabeth were married at Marylebone.

Since he did not want her to go on earning a living as a singer, he had to try and find a way of making money quickly. Naturally, he turned to the theatre, for his father had written a successful farce and his mother, several comedies. He was encouraged in this by Thomas Harris, principal manager of Covent Garden Theatre and a shrewd judge of actors and dramatists. On 17 November 1774, Sheridan was able to write to his father-in-law to say: 'There will be a comedy of mine in rehearsal at Covent-Garden within a few days.' He added proudly that he had 'not written a line of it two months ago, except a scene or two, which I believe you have seen in an odd act of a little farce'.

The Covent Garden company had scored its greatest recent success in Goldsmith's *She Stoops to Conquer* (15 March 1773), and had gone on acting it, from time to time, ever since. Before Sheridan completed *The Rivals*, he could have seen the company in *She Stoops* on two occasions, 21 September and 8 November. We do not know that he did so, but it is interesting to speculate what the effect on him would have been, for *The Rivals*, like *She Stoops*, is a comedy based on farce and theatrical types. It is even more thought-provoking to observe that three of the actors and two of the actresses from this cast were also to take part in the first performance of *The Rivals*. Edward Shuter played droll old gentlemen, so he was Mr. Hardcastle and Sir Anthony. John Quick played young, countrified squires, and was a natural Tony Lumpkin as well as Bob Acres. Lee Lewes liked portraying the slightly arrogant, and took Young Marlow and Fag. Mrs. Green shone as the would-be gentlewoman full of airs and graces, so she created Mrs. Hardcastle and Mrs. Malaprop. Mrs.

Bulkley excelled as the lively, open young woman, so was Kate Hardcastle and Julia.

Within a year Sheridan was to show how carefully he studied the capabilities of the likely performers in his plays when fitting out parts for them to act, and it seems likely that he took the same attitude now. Of course, there were several leading members of the cast of *The Rivals* who were not in *She Stoops*, but he could easily have noted their particular talents by a few nights' attendance at the playhouse. Henry Woodward, who played Jack Absolute, had recently acted Mercutio. W. T. Lewis (Faulkland) had been seen as Romeo, and John Lee (Sir Lucius), as Benedick.

The first performance of *The Rivals* took place on 17 January 1775, and was not a success. Sir Joshua Reynolds's nephew, writing a few weeks later, said it 'but just escaped' damnation, 'though some people admire it'. This ambiguous result was caused partly by the play itself and partly by the incompetence of some of the actors. The prompter could be heard constantly when Shuter and Lee were on stage, and Lee was undoubtedly miscast as Sir Lucius. The comedy was criticized as being much too long and containing weak puns and coarse innuendoes.

The play might never have been performed again, but Thomas Harris was still enthusiastic and he insisted on Sheridan's revising it in the light of these criticisms. Fortunately the twenty-three-year-old dramatist was to show considerable talent as a 'play doctor', and he saw just how the comedy could be improved. Later he said he looked upon the first-night audience as 'a candid and judicious friend attending in behalf of the public, at his last rehearsal'. That was more than an excuse for his own inexperience: it was an acknowledgement of what an audience could teach a young playwright about the nature of his craft and the taste of the day.

His own admiration for Congreve's *The Old Bachelor* (1693) and Vanbrugh's *The Relapse* (1696) had been evident, but he now had to learn that the wildness and freedom of speech of Restoration dramatists were no longer socially acceptable. He must capture their gusto without their grossness. He must remember that a mid-eighteenth century audience prided itself on its decorum, sensibility, and critical perception. So some of the coarseness associated with Sir Anthony's part and the more bizarre word-play given to Acres and Mrs. Malaprop, were deleted. Sir Lucius was converted from a rather stupid fortune-hunter into a peremptory man of honour. Some scenes were removed, some speeches tightened, and the whole play was subtly given a more definite shape.

The revised version was presented on 28 January with the same cast, except for Lee. His place was taken by Laurence Clinch, a newcomer to the company but an old friend of the Sheridans. Loud applause greeted his Sir Lucius, and the play was generally admired. David Garrick, manager of the rival theatre, remarked early in the evening, 'I see this play will creep.' At the end he had to say, 'I see this play will run.'

It has been consistently successful ever since, and it is not difficult to understand why it has achieved such a place in the repertory. For one thing, it is full of the vitality, and the exaggerations, of youth. Acres and Mrs. Malaprop use language oddly but with great spirit. Sir Lucius and Lydia behave capriciously according to some high-flown code of their own. All four struggle to live in a world of their own making, and are fit subjects for laughter because their self-satisfaction is not justified. Yet while they may be foolish in some respects, they are by no means fools, and the process of stripping them of their self-regard is accompanied by felicities of language as well as verbal oddities.

The dialogue of the comic scenes is very well turned, and has a jauntiness and an ingenuity that come over superbly.

The play has, too, a neat plot that develops amusingly and very clearly. The scenes move on briskly to make their points. Jack's downright refusal to marry the girl his father chooses for him, changes to eager acquiescence as soon as he finds that she is his adored Lydia, and to equal dismay when she objects to anything but a romantic elopement. Similarly, Sir Anthony demands that his son should give him implicit obedience, but is far from satisfied when Jack says that he is willing to marry niece or aunt:

SIR ANTHONY: ... The aunt, indeed! Odds life! when I ran away with your mother, I would not have touched anything old or ugly to gain an empire.
ABSOLUTE: Not to please your father, sir?

This ability to turn the situation completely is one of Sheridan's great gifts, and in this example and a few others, the reversals spring from character.

In neither farce nor comedy of manners is it really necessary to develop character, for the interest of the one depends on situation and that of the other on ridiculing unusual behaviour. Consequently Malaprop, Languish, and O'Trigger, are merely what their names suggest. Only one relationship is developed beyond the requirements of the plot: that between father and son is touched in with a nice irony and a rich humour. In fact, their scenes have an imaginative force that makes them stand out in the theatre.

This is also the place to appreciate best the Julia/Faulkland scenes that appear so mawkish to modern readers. The eighteenth-century audience was moved by them, and the *Morning Post*, 24 January 1775, wrote that 'the exquisite refinement in his [Faulkland's] disposition, opposed to the noble simplicity, tenderness, and candour of Julia's, give rise to some of the most affecting sentimental scenes'. Julia still has all these virtues, but Faulkland seems fretful, and his language artificial, to the point of mania. Yet, watching him on the stage, we can make allowances: he is in love, and lovers are commonly jealous, prickly, and tiresome people. Although the prologue for the tenth night suggests that mockery of 'the Sentimental Muse' was intended, no one can see the play without perceiving that while Sheridan laughed at Faulkland, he also luxuriated in his feverish sensibility. The reason is obvious: in Sheridan's own temperament there was an uneasy mixture of the satirical and the sentimental. In this comedy he was to reconcile these opposites to brilliant effect.

A NOTE ON THE TEXT

THE text is taken from the 'third edition corrected' (1776), as presented by Sheridan to Garrick and now in the Dyce Collection of the Library of the Victoria and Albert Museum. I am indebted to the Librarian for permitting me to reproduce the half-title showing the presentation inscription.

In reproducing the text, I have modernized the spelling. This means that '-'d' becomes '-ed' (except in 'd-n'd', which is retained to give period flavour), and that certain correct eighteenth-century spellings are given modern form: 'by the by' (in place of 'by the bye'), 'stupefy' ('stupify'), 'sofa' ('sopha'), 'chooses' ('chuses'), 'showed' ('shew'd'), 'paduasoy' ('padusoy'), 'frenzy' ('phrenzy'), 'skulking' ('sculking'). I have retained an old spelling in 'tho'ff', which seems to indicate a dialect pronunciation, and in the title of Smollett's novel, *Humphry Clinker*.

I have normalized the capitalization, so avoiding the arbitrary usage of the eighteenth century, but in the matter of punctuation, I have followed eighteenth-century practice as far as possible. I do so to suggest the elaborate breath-pauses of the period. Italics have been retained for emphasis.

The text of the prologue for the first night has not been printed in any other edition of *The Rivals*, and was thought to be irretrievably lost. Fortunately it has come to light in the Amelia Edwards Collection of Somerville College, Oxford, and I am grateful to the Librarian, Mrs. Norma Russell, for permission to copy and print it. I include, too, the preface that was printed in the first and second editions of *The Rivals*, but not in the 'third edition corrected'. Two of the songs in II.i, are now identified. See p. 139.

SOME DATES IN SHERIDAN'S LIFE

4 Nov. 1751. Christened 'Thos. Brinsley Sheridan' at St. Mary's Church, Dublin.

1762–c.1767–8. At Harrow School.

Sept. 1770–Aug. 1772. At Bath.

Aug. 1772–March 1773. At Waltham Abbey.

13 April 1773. Married Elizabeth Linley.

17 and 28 Jan. 1775. *The Rivals* acted at Covent Garden Theatre.

2 May 1775. *St. Patrick's Day* acted at Covent Garden Theatre.

21 Nov. 1775. *The Duenna* acted at Covent Garden Theatre.

21 Sept. 1776. Opened Drury Lane Theatre as principal manager.

24 Feb. 1777. Put on *A Trip to Scarborough* (his revision of Vanbrugh's *The Relapse*) at Drury Lane Theatre.

8 May 1777. *The School for Scandal* acted at Drury Lane Theatre.

30 Oct. 1779. *The Critic* acted at Drury Lane Theatre.

12 Sept. 1780. Elected M.P. for Stafford.

1782. Became Under-Secretary of State for Foreign Affairs.

1783. Became Secretary to the Treasury.

Dec. 1783–Feb. 1806. In Opposition.

1806–7. Treasurer of the Navy in the Ministry of All the Talents.

24 Feb. 1809. Drury Lane Theatre destroyed by fire.

Autumn 1812. Lost his seat in Parliament.

7 July 1816. Died at Saville Row.

13 July 1816. Buried in Westminster Abbey.

BOOKS FOR FURTHER READING

Thomas Moore, *Memoirs of the Life of the Right Honourable Richard Brinsley Sheridan* (5th ed., 1827, 2 vols.)
This is still the best biography of Sheridan.

The Plays and Poems of Richard Brinsley Sheridan. Ed. R. Crompton Rhodes, Oxford, 1928; repr., New York, 1962; 3 vols.
The most comprehensive collection of Sheridan's works.

The Rivals, A Comedy. Edited from the Larpent MS. by Richard Little Purdy, Oxford, 1935.
Prints the manuscript first version of the play (as sent to the Lord Chamberlain) side by side with the first printed edition. A judicious introduction is also included.

British Dramatists from Dryden to Sheridan. Edited by G. H. Nettleton and A. E. Case, 1939.
Includes good texts of *The Rivals, The School for Scandal*, and *The Critic*, as well as representative plays of the period.

The Letters of Richard Brinsley Sheridan. Edited by Cecil Price, Oxford, 1966, 3 vols.
Volume I contains (pp. 84–95) Sheridan's letters on *The Rivals* and *The Duenna*. See also Volume III, 292–3.

J. O. Bartley, *Teague, Shenkin, and Sawney*, Cork, 1954.
For the development of the stage Irishman.

The London Stage, 1660–1800: Part 4: 1747–1776. Edited by G. W. Stone, Jr., Carbondale, 1962, 3 vols.
An invaluable calendar of all London stage performances of the period.

Johnson's England. Edited by A. S. Turberville, Oxford, 1933; repr. 1965; 2 vols.

An account of the life and manners of the age, with a chapter on drama and theatre.

Tobias Smollett, *The Expedition of Humphry Clinker*. Edited by L. M. Knapp, Oxford, 1965.

This gives a satirical picture of life at Bath in the eighteenth century, then goes on to describe a tour in Britain.

Mary E. Knapp, *Prologues and Epilogues of the Eighteenth Century*, New Haven, 1961.

A careful analysis of their content and what is revealed of the taste of the audience.

A Barbeau, *Life and Letters at Bath in the XVIIIth Century*, 1904.

Dave'd Garrick Esq
From The Author

THE

R I V A L S.

A

C O M E D Y.

[Price One Shilling and Sixpence.]

The half-title of the third edition of *The Rivals*, with Sheridan's presentation inscription to David Garrick. The copy is in the Dyce collection at the Victoria and Albert Museum, London, and the page is reproduced by permission of the Librarian.

THE RIVALS

A COMEDY

Preface

A PREFACE to a play seems generally to be considered as a kind of closet-prologue, in which—if his piece has been successful—the author solicits that indulgence from the reader which he had before experienced from the audience: but as the scope and immediate object of a play is to please a mixed assembly in *representation* (whose judgment in the theatre at least is decisive) its degree of reputation is usually as determined as public, before it can be prepared for the cooler tribunal of the study. Thus any farther solicitude on the part of the writer becomes unnecessary at least, if not an intrusion: and if the piece has been condemned in the performance, I fear an address to the closet, like an appeal to posterity, is constantly regarded as the procrastination of a suit, from a consciousness of the weakness of the cause. From these considerations, the following comedy would certainly have been submitted to the reader, without any further introduction than what it had in the representation, but that its success has probably been founded on a circumstance which the author is informed has not before attended a theatrical trial, and which consequently ought not to pass unnoticed.

I need scarcely add, that the circumstance alluded to, was the withdrawing of the piece, to remove those imperfections in the first representation which were too obvious to escape reprehension, and too numerous to admit of a hasty correction. There are few writers, I believe, who, even in the fullest consciousness of error, do not wish to palliate the faults which they acknowledge; and, however trifling the performance, to second their confession of its deficiencies, by whatever plea seems least disgraceful to their ability. In the present instance, it cannot be said to amount either to candour or modesty in me, to acknowledge an extreme inexperience and want of judgment on matters, in which, without guidance from practice, or spur from success, a young man should scarcely boast of being an adept. If it be said, that under such disadvantages no one should attempt to write a play—I must beg leave to dissent from the position, while the first point of experience that I have gained on the subject is, a knowledge of the candour and judgment with which an impartial public distinguishes between the errors of inexperience and incapacity, and the indulgence which it shews even to a disposition to remedy the defects of either.

It were unnecessary to enter into any farther extenuation of what was thought exceptionable in this play, but that it has been said, that the managers should have prevented some of the defects before its appearance to the public—and in particular the uncommon length of the piece as represented the first night.—It were an ill return for the most liberal and gentlemanly conduct on their side, to suffer any censure to rest where none was deserved. Hurry in writing has long been exploded as an excuse for an author;—however, in the dramatic line, it may happen, that both an author and a manager may wish to fill a chasm in the entertainment of the public with a hastiness not altogether culpable. The season was advanced when I first put the play into Mr. Harris's hands:—it was at that time at least double the length of any acting comedy.—I profited by his judgment and experience in the curtailing of it—'till, I believe, his feeling for the vanity of a young author got the better of his desire for correctness, and he left many excrescences remaining, because he had assisted in pruning so many more. Hence, though I was not uninformed that the acts were still too long, I flattered myself that, after the first trial, I might with safer judgment proceed to remove what should appear to have been most dissatisfactory.—Many other errors there were, which might in part have arisen from my being by no means conversant with plays in general, either in reading or at the theatre.—Yet I own that, in one respect, I did not regret my ignorance: for as my first wish in attempting a play, was to avoid every appearance of plagiary, I thought I should stand a better chance of effecting this from being in a walk which I had not frequented, and where consequently the progress of invention was less likely to be interrupted by starts of recollection: for on subjects on which the mind has been much informed, invention is slow of exerting itself.—Faded ideas float in the fancy like half-forgotten dreams; and the imagination in its fullest enjoyments becomes suspicious of its offspring, and doubts whether it has created or adopted.

With regard to some particular passages which on the first night's representation seemed generally disliked, I confess, that if I felt any emotion of surprise at the disapprobation, it was not that they were disapproved of, but that I had not before perceived that they deserved it. As some part of the attack on the piece was begun too early to pass for the sentence of *judgment*, which is ever tardy in condemning, it has been suggested to me, that much of the disapprobation must have arisen from virulence of malice, rather than severity of criticism: but as I was more apprehensive of there being just grounds to excite the latter, than conscious of having deserved the former, I continue not to believe that probable, which I am sure must have been unprovoked. However, if it was so, and I could even mark the quarter from whence it came, it would be ungenerous to retort; for no passion suffers more than malice from disappointment. For my own part, I see no reason why the author of a play should not regard a first night's audience, as a candid and judicious friend attending, in behalf of the public, at his last rehearsal. If he can dispense with flattery, he is sure at least of sincerity, and even though the annotation be rude, he may rely upon the justness of the comment. Considered in this light, that audience whose *fiat* is essential to the poet's claim, whether his object be fame or profit, has surely a right to expect some deference to its opinion, from principles of politeness at least, if not from gratitude.

As for the little puny critics, who scatter their peevish strictures in private circles, and scribble at every author who has the eminence of being unconnected with them, as they are usually spleen-swollen from a vain idea of increasing their consequence, there will always be found a petulance and illiberality in their remarks, which should place them as far beneath the notice of a gentleman, as their original dulness had sunk them from the level of the most unsuccessful author.

It is not without pleasure that I catch at an opportunity of justifying myself from the charge of intending any national reflection in the character of Sir *Lucius O'Trigger*. If any gentlemen opposed the piece from that idea, I thank them sincerely for their opposition; and if the condemnation of this comedy (however misconceived the provocation,) could have added one spark to the decaying flame of national attachment to the country supposed to be reflected on, I should have been happy in its fate; and might with truth have boasted, that it had done more real service in its failure, than the successful morality of a thousand stage-novels will ever effect.

It is usual, I believe, to thank the performers in a new play, for the exertion of their several abilities. But where (as in this instance) their merit has been so striking and uncontroverted, as to call for the warmest and truest applause from a number of judicious audiences, the poet's after-praise comes like the feeble acclamation of a child to close the shouts of a multitude. The conduct, however, of the principals in a theatre cannot be so apparent to the public.—I think it therefore but justice to declare, that from this theatre (the only one I can speak of from experience), those writers who wish to try the dramatic line, will meet with that candour and liberal attention, which are generally allowed to be better calculated to lead genius into excellence, than either the precepts of judgment, or the guidance of experience.

THE AUTHOR.

DRAMATIS PERSONAE

As originally acted at Covent Garden Theatre
on 17 January 1775

Men

SIR ANTHONY ABSOLUTE	Mr. Shuter
CAPTAIN ABSOLUTE	Mr. Woodward
FAULKLAND	Mr. Lewis
ACRES	Mr. Quick
SIR LUCIUS O'TRIGGER	Mr. Lee
FAG	Mr. Lee Lewes
DAVID	Mr. Dunstall
COACHMAN	Mr. Fearon

Women

MRS. MALAPROP	Mrs. Green
LYDIA LANGUISH	Miss Barsanti
JULIA	Mrs. Bulkley
LUCY	Mrs. Lessingham

Maid, Boy, Servants, &c.
SCENE—*Bath*.
Time of Action, within One Day.[1]

[1] The first edition reads: 'Time of Action, Five Hours.'

PROLOGUE

By the Author

Enter SERJEANT-AT-LAW *and* ATTORNEY *following and giving a paper*

SERJEANT: What's here—a vile cramp hand! I cannot see
  Without my spectacles.

ATTORNEY: He means his fee.[1]

. . . .[2]

—They'll either clear the sight—or serve as blinkers.

SERJEANT: How's this?—a *poet's* brief?

ATTORNEY: Aye even so:—

SERJEANT: The deuce!—a *poet* and a *fee*!—O ho!—
  Some noble writer I suppose?—

ATTORNEY: Oh! No!
  A student erring from the Temple's bounds
  Pleads to a trespass on the Muse's grounds.

SERJEANT: Ill fare the truant who with giddy haste
  Forsakes an *orchard*—for a barren *waste*!

ATTORNEY: Nor pleads *He* worse—who with a decent sprig
  Of bays—adorns his legal waste of wig:
  Full bottomed heroes thus, on signs, unfurl
  A leaf of laurel in a grove of curl!

SERJEANT: Yet tell your client that in *adverse* days,
  This wig—is warmer than a bush of bays:
  And tell him too—how hard it is to deal
  With that dread court—from whence there's no appeal!

[1] The opening lines are missing in the Somerville College MS., so everything preceding 'fee' is taken from the prologue that was given on the second night.
[2] Missing. I invent the following to suggest the sense:
    'For spectacles well suit such pretty thinkers.'

No tricking there—to blunt the edge of *law*,
Or, damn'd in *equity*, escape by—*flaw*:—
But *judgment* given—their sentence must remain!—
No *writ of error* lies to—*Drury-Lane*!

ATTORNEY: Do you then, sir, our student's place supply:—
Profuse of robe, and prodigal of tie—
Do you—with all those blushing pow'rs of face,
And wonted bashful hesitating grace
Rise in the court—and flourish on the case. *Exit* ATTORNEY

SERJEANT: For practice then—suppose—(this brief will show
it)—
Me—Serjeant *Lewis*[1]—counsel for the poet:
But first—lest partial spleen our words pervert—
My client's *right of challenge* I'll exert.
—Above—below—in jackets silk—or flannel—
Hissers of all kind I—strike off the panel.—[*looking round*]
No!—no such thing!—no spite!—no hoarded fury!
—I think I never faced—a milder *jury*!
Sad else our plight—where frowns are—*transportation*!
A *hiss*—the *gallows*!—and a *groan*—*damnation*![2]
But from so mild a court—'tis past dispute
He'll gain *some favour*—if not costs of suit.
There's one thing only I shall mention more—[*going*]
—This culprit—ne'er was at your bar before:
Of all intruders should he prove the worst,
Forgive the trespass—since it is the FIRST

---

[1] W. T. Lewis (1748?–1811) acted the part of Faulkland, and may have taken the Serjeant, too. *The Town and Country Magazine*, Jan. 1775, suggests that Lee performed the Serjeant. A third possibility is that the part was acted by Lee Lewes.

[2] The play was nearly damned on the first night, so Sheridan carefully revised the prologue for the second performance.

PROLOGUE

By the Author

Spoken on the Tenth Night, by Mrs. Bulkley

GRANTED our cause, our suit and trial o'er,
The worthy serjeant need appear no more:
In pleasing I a different client choose,
He served the Poet—I would serve the Muse:
Like him, I'll try to merit your applause,
A female counsel in a female's cause.

Look on this form[1]—where humour, quaint and sly,
Dimples the cheek, and points the beaming eye;
Where gay Invention seems to boast its wiles
In amorous hint, and half-triumphant smiles;
While her light mask or[2] covers Satire's strokes,
All hides the conscious blush her wit provokes.
—Look on her well—does she seem formed to teach?
Should you *expect* to hear this lady—preach?
Is grey experience suited to her youth?
Do solemn sentiments become that mouth?
Bid her be grave, those lips should rebel prove
To every theme that slanders mirth or love.

Yet thus adorned with every graceful art
To charm the fancy and yet reach the heart —
Must we displace her? And instead advance
The goddess of the woeful countenance—
The sentimental Muse!—Her emblems view,
The Pilgrim's Progress, and a sprig of rue!
View her—too chaste to look like flesh and blood—

[1] Pointing to the figure of Comedy in Covent Garden Theatre.
[2] O'er?

Primly portrayed on emblematic wood!
There fixed in usurpation should she stand,
She'll snatch the dagger from her sister's hand:
And having made her vot'ries *weep a flood*,
Good heav'n! she'll end her comedies in blood—
Bid *Harry Woodward* break poor *Dunstall's* crown!
Imprison *Quick*—and knock *Ned Shuter* down;
While sad *Barsanti*—weeping o'er the scene—
Shall stab herself—or poison Mrs. *Green*.—

Such dire encroachments to prevent in time,
Demands the critic's voice—the poet's rhyme.
Can our light scenes add strength to holy laws?
Such puny patronage but hurts the cause:
Fair Virtue scorns our feeble aid to ask;
And moral Truth disdains the trickster's mask.
For here their fav'rite stands,[1] whose brow—severe
And sad—claims Youth's respect, and Pity's tear;
Who—when oppressed by foes her worth creates—
Can point a poniard at the guilt she hates.

---

[1] Pointing to the figure of Tragedy.

Act I scene i

A street in Bath

COACHMAN *crosses the stage.—Enter* FAG,
looking after him

FAG: What!—Thomas!—Sure, 'tis he?—What!—Thomas!
—Thomas!

COACHMAN: Hey!—Odd's life![1]—Mr. Fag!—give us your
hand, my old fellow-servant.

FAG: Excuse my glove, Thomas:—I'm dev'lish glad to see   5
you, my lad: why, my prince of charioteers, you look as
hearty!—but who the deuce thought of seeing you in
Bath!

COACHMAN: Sure, Master, Madam Julia, Harry, Mrs. Kate,
and the postillion be all come!   10

FAG: Indeed!

COACHMAN: Aye! Master thought another fit of the gout
was coming to make him a visit:—so he'd a mind to gi't
the slip, and whip! we were all off at an hour's warning.

FAG: Aye, aye! hasty in everything, or it would not be Sir   15
Anthony Absolute!

COACHMAN: But tell us, Mr. Fag, how does young master?
Odd! Sir Anthony will stare to see the Captain here!

FAG: I do not serve Captain Absolute now.—

COACHMAN: Why sure!   20

FAG: At present I am employed by Ensign[2] Beverley.

[1] Probably a corruption of 'God's life', as in "'slife'.
[2] The most junior infantry officer, who carried the colours in battle.

COACHMAN: I doubt, Mr. Fag, you ha'n't changed for the better.

FAG: I have not changed, Thomas.

COACHMAN: No! why, didn't you say you had left young   25 master?

FAG: No.—Well, honest Thomas, I must puzzle you no farther:—briefly then—Capt. Absolute and Ensign Beverley are one and the same person.

COACHMAN: The devil they are!   30

FAG: So it is indeed, Thomas; and the *Ensign*-half of my master being on guard at present—the *Captain* has nothing to do with me.

COACHMAN: So, so!—What, this is some freak, I warrant! —Do, tell us, Mr Fag, the meaning o't—you know I ha'   35 trusted you.

FAG: You'll be secret, Thomas?

COACHMAN: As a coach-horse.

FAG: Why then the cause of all this is—LOVE,—Love, Thomas, who (as you may get read to you) has been a   40 masquerader ever since the days of Jupiter. [1]

COACHMAN: Aye, aye;—I guessed there was a lady in the case:—but pray, why does your master pass only for *Ensign?*—Now if he had shammed *General*, indeed—

FAG: Ah! Thomas, there lies the mystery o' the matter.—   45 Hark'ee, Thomas, my master is in love with a lady of a very singular[2] taste: a lady who likes him better as a *half-pay*[3] *Ensign* than if she knew he was son and heir to Sir Anthony Absolute, a baronet of three thousand a-year!

---

[1] The most powerful of the classical gods changed himself into a bull and a swan in his pursuit of women. One of Sheridan's earliest attempts at a play was *Jupiter* (or *Ixion*), which he wrote in collaboration with his friend N. B. Halhed. It showed Jupiter coming down to earth to woo Major Amphitryon's wife.

[2] Odd.

[3] Drawing half his allowance because he was not on active service.

COACHMAN: That is an odd taste indeed!—but has she got   50
the stuff, Mr. Fag? is she rich, hey?

FAG: Rich!—why, I believe she owns half the stocks![1]—
Z—ds![2] Thomas, she could pay the national debt as easily
as I could my washerwoman!—She has a lap-dog that eats
out of gold,—she feeds her parrot with small pearls,—and   55
all her thread-papers[3] are made of bank-notes!

COACHMAN: Bravo!—Faith!—Odd! I warrant she has a set
of thousands[4] at least:—but does she draw kindly[5] with
the Captain?

FAG: As fond as pigeons.[6]   60

COACHMAN: May one hear her name?

FAG: Miss Lydia Languish.—But there is an old tough
aunt in the way;—though, by the by—she has never seen
my master—for he got acquainted with Miss while on a
visit in Gloucestershire.   65

COACHMAN: Well—I wish they were once harnessed
together in matrimony.—But pray, Mr. Fag, what kind
of a place is this Bath?—I ha' heard a deal of it—here's a
mort[7] o'merry-making—hey?

FAG: Pretty well, Thomas, pretty well—'tis a good lounge;[8]   70
in the morning we go to the pump-room (though neither
my master nor I drink the waters); after breakfast we
saunter on the parades or play a game at billiards; at night
we dance: but d—n the place, I'm tired of it: their regular
hours stupefy me—not a fiddle nor a card after eleven!—   75
However, Mr. Faulkland's gentleman and I keep it up a
little in private parties;—I'll introduce you there, Thomas
—you'll like him much.

---

[1] Money lent to the government.   [2] A corruption of 'God's wounds'.
[3] Soft paper used for rolling up skeins of thread.
[4] Thread-papers worth thousands.
[5] The analogy is with a horse and mare pulling together in the shafts of a coach.
[6] The turtle-doves of poetry and romance: cf. p. 139.
[7] Dialect for 'a great amount'.   [8] Place for relaxing.

COACHMAN: Sure I know Mr. Du-Peigne[1]—you know   80
his master is to marry Madam Julia.

FAG: I had forgot.—But Thomas you must polish a little—
indeed you must.—Here now—this wig! what the devil
do you do with a *wig*, Thomas?—none of the London
whips of any degree of *ton*[2] wear *wigs* now.

COACHMAN: More's the pity! more's the pity, I say—Odd's   85
life! when I heard how the lawyers and doctors had took
to their own hair, I thought how 'twould go next:—Odd
rabbit it![3] when the fashion had got foot on the Bar, I
guessed 'twould mount to the Box![4]—But 'tis all out of
character, believe me, Mr. Fag: and look'ee, I'll never gi'   90
up mine—the lawyers and doctors may do as they will.

FAG: Well, Thomas, we'll not quarrel about that.

COACHMAN: Why, bless you, the gentlemen of they pro-
fessions ben't all of a mind—for in our village now, tho'ff[5]
Jack Gauge, the *exciseman*,[6] has ta'en to his carrots,[7] there's 95
little Dick, the farrier,[8] swears he'll never forsake his *bob*,[9]
tho' all the college[10] should appear with their own heads!

FAG: Indeed! well said, Dick! But hold—mark! mark!
Thomas.

COACHMAN: Zooks![11] 'tis the Captain!—Is that the lady   100
with him?

FAG: No! no! that is Madam Lucy—my master's mistress's

---

[1] He of the comb: a French valet. Cf. De-la-Grace, the dancing-master (p. 85),
and La Vérole in Vanbrugh's *The Relapse* (1696).

[2] Men of fashion gave up wigs, and began powdering their hair.

[3] Probably a genteel way of saying 'God rot it'.

[4] Fashion would force coachmen to follow the example of legal gentlemen.

[5] Though.

[6] Customs officers measured the contents of casks. 'Gage, an exciseman', is a
character in a later play that Sheridan had a hand in: *The Camp*, acted in 1778.

[7] His own red hair.   [8] Animal doctor.

[9] Bob-wig: it kept close to the head and had short curls at the nape.

[10] Professional institution to which doctors belong.

[11] 'Gadzooks!', an exclamation, though once an oath.

maid.—They lodge at that house—but I must after him to tell him the news.

COACHMAN: Odd! he's giving her money!—well, Mr. 105 Fag—

FAG: Good-bye, Thomas.—I have an appointment in Gyde's Porch[1] this evening at eight; meet me there, and we'll make a little party.

Exeunt severally

Scene ii

A Dressing-room in MRS. MALAPROP'S *lodgings*

LYDIA *sitting on a sofa, with a book in her hand.—*
LUCY, *has just returned from a message*

LUCY: Indeed, ma'am, I traversed half the town in search of it:—I don't believe there's a circulating library[2] in Bath I ha'n't been at.

LYDIA: And could you not get *The Reward of Constancy*?[3]

LUCY: No, indeed, ma'am.   5

LYDIA: Nor *The Fatal Connexion*?

LUCY: No, indeed, ma'am.

LYDIA: Nor *The Mistakes of the Heart*?

LUCY: Ma'am, as ill-luck would have it, Mr. Bull[4] said Miss Sukey Saunter had just fetched it away.   10

LYDIA: Heigh-ho!—Did you inquire for *The Delicate Distress*?—

---

[1] Gyde's Assembly rooms were on the Lower Walks.

[2] A bookseller's collection lent out on payment of a fee.

[3] The list of books mentioned by Lydia and Lucy is given on p. 137.

[4] Lewis Bull, a Bath bookseller.

LUCY: Or *The Memoirs of Lady Woodford*? Yes indeed,
ma'am.—I asked everywhere for it; and I might have
brought it from Mr. Frederick's,[1] but Lady Slattern   15
Lounger, who had just sent it home, had so soiled and
dog's-eared[2] it, it wa'n't fit for a Christian to read.

LYDIA: Heigh-ho!—Yes, I always know when Lady
Slattern has been before me.—She has a most observing
thumb; and I believe cherishes her nails for the conveni-   20
ence of making marginal notes.—Well, child,[3] what *have*
you brought me?

LUCY: Oh! here, ma'am. [*Taking books from under her cloak,
and from her pockets*] This is *The Gordian Knot*,—and this
Peregrine Pickle. Here are *The Tears of Sensibility*, and   25
Humphry Clinker. This is *The Memoirs of a Lady of Quality,
written by herself*,—and here the second volume of *The
Sentimental Journey*.

LYDIA: Heigh-ho!—What are those books by the glass?

LUCY: The great one is only *The Whole Duty of Man*—   30
where I press a few blonds,[4] ma'am.

LYDIA: Very well—give me the *sal volatile*.[5]

LUCY: Is it in a blue cover, ma'am?

LYDIA: My smelling bottle, you simpleton!

LUCY: Oh, the drops!—Here, ma'am.   35

LYDIA: Hold!—here's some one coming—quick! see who
it is.—   *Exit* LUCY
Surely I heard my cousin Julia's voice!

[1] William Frederick, another Bath bookseller. In the *Bath Journal*, 24 Sept. 1770,
he said he was giving up his circulating library.

[2] The top corner of the page turned down to show where the reader had
stopped.

[3] She appears to be only a little younger than her mistress, but Lydia shows her
a kindly condescension.

[4] Silk lace.

[5] A solution of ammonium carbonate sometimes drunk as sal volatile or, as
crystals, sniffed as smelling salts. Both were restoratives to ward off faintness or
headaches.

Re-enter LUCY

LUCY: Lud! ma'am, here is Miss Melville.
LYDIA: Is it possible!——   40

Enter JULIA

LYDIA: My dearest Julia, how delighted am I!—[*Embrace*]
How unexpected was this happiness!
JULIA: True, Lydia—and our pleasure is the greater;—but
what has been the matter?—you were denied to me at
first!   45
LYDIA: Ah! Julia, I have a thousand things to tell you!—but
first inform me, what has conjured[1] you to Bath?—Is Sir
Anthony here?
JULIA: He is—we are arrived within this hour—and I suppose he will be here to wait on Mrs. Malaprop as soon as   50
he is dressed.[2]
LYDIA: Then before we are interrupted, let me impart to
you some of my distress!—I know your gentle nature will
sympathize with me, tho' your prudence may condemn
me!—My letters have informed you of my whole con-   55
nection with Beverley;—but I have lost him, Julia!—my
aunt has discovered our intercourse by a note she intercepted, and has confined me ever since!—Yet, would you
believe it? she has fallen absolutely in love with a tall
Irish baronet she met one night since we have been here,   60
at Lady Macshuffle's rout.[3]
JULIA: You jest, Lydia!
LYDIA: No, upon my word.—She really carries on a kind of
correspondence with him, under a feigned name though,

---

[1] Brought by magical compulsion.
[2] Put on formal (as distinct from travelling) clothes.   [3] Party.

till she chooses to be known to him;—but it is a *Delia* or a   65
Celia,[1] I assure you.

JULIA: Then, surely, she is now more indulgent to her
niece.

LYDIA: Quite the contrary. Since she has discovered her own
frailty she is become more suspicious of mine. Then I   70
must inform you of another plague!—That odious *Acres*
is to be in Bath to-day; so that I protest I shall be teased
out of all spirits!

JULIA: Come, come, Lydia, hope the best.—Sir Anthony
shall use his interest with Mrs. Malaprop.   75

LYDIA: But you have not heard the worst. Unfortunately
I had quarrelled with my poor Beverley, just before my
aunt made the discovery, and I have not seen him since, to
make it up.

JULIA: What was his offence?   80

LYDIA: Nothing at all!—But, I don't know how it was, as
often as we had been together, we had never had a quarrel!
—And, somehow, I was afraid he would never give me an
opportunity.—So, last Thursday, I wrote a letter to myself, to inform myself that Beverley was at that time   85
paying his addresses to another woman.—I signed it *your
Friend unknown*, showed it to Beverley, charged him with
his falsehood, put myself in a violent passion, and vowed
I'd never see him more.

JULIA: And you let him depart so, and have not seen him   90
since?

LYDIA: 'Twas the next day my aunt found the matter out.
I intended only to have teased him three days and a half,
and now I've lost him for ever!

JULIA: If he is as deserving and sincere as you have repre-   95
sented him to me, he will never give you up so. Yet con-

---

[1] Names much used in love poetry of the previous hundred years, and so
fashionable in courtship.

sider, Lydia, you tell me he is but an ensign, and you have
thirty thousand pounds!

LYDIA: But you know I lose most of my fortune if I marry
without my aunt's consent, till of age; and that is what I   100
have determined to do, ever since I knew the penalty.—
Nor could I love the man, who would wish to wait a day
for the alternative.

JULIA: Nay, this is caprice!

LYDIA: What, does Julia tax me with caprice?—I thought   105
her lover Faulkland had enured her to it.

JULIA: I do not love even *his* faults.

LYDIA: But a-propos[1]—you have sent to him, I suppose?

JULIA: Not yet, upon my word—nor has he the least idea
of my being in Bath.—Sir Anthony's resolution was so   110
sudden, I could not inform him of it.

LYDIA: Well, Julia, you are your own mistress (though
under the protection of Sir Anthony), yet have you for
this long year, been a slave to the caprice, the whim, the
jealousy of this ungrateful Faulkland, who will ever delay   115
assuming the right of a husband, while you suffer him to
be equally imperious as a lover.

JULIA: Nay, you are wrong entirely.—We were contracted
before my father's death.—That, and some consequent
embarrassments, have delayed what I know to be my   120
Faulkland's most ardent wish.—He is too generous to
trifle on such a point.—And for his character, you wrong
him there too.—No, Lydia, he is too proud, too noble to
be jealous; if he is captious, 'tis without dissembling; if
fretful, without rudeness.—Unused to the fopperies[2] of   125
love, he is negligent of the little duties expected from a
lover—but being unhackneyed[3] in the passion, his affection is ardent and sincere; and as it engrosses his whole

---

[1] On the subject we are discussing.
[2] Petty refinements.   [3] Not over-accustomed to.

soul, he expects every thought and emotion of his mistress
to move in unison with his.—Yet, though his pride calls   130
for this full return—his humility makes him undervalue
those qualities in him, which would entitle him to it; and
not feeling why he should be loved to the degree he
wishes, he still suspects that he is not loved enough.—This
temper, I must own, has cost me many unhappy hours;   135
but I have learned to think myself his debtor, for those
imperfections which arise from the ardour of his attachment.

LYDIA: Well, I cannot blame you for defending him.—But
tell me candidly, Julia, had he never saved your life, do   140
you think you should have been attached to him as you
are?—Believe me, the rude blast that overset your boat
was a prosperous gale of love to him.

JULIA: Gratitude may have strengthened my attachment to
Mr. Faulkland, but I loved him before he had preserved   145
me; yet surely that alone were an obligation sufficient—

LYDIA: Obligation?—Why, a water-spaniel would have
done as much.—Well, I should never think of giving my
heart to a man because he could swim!

JULIA: Come, Lydia, you are too inconsiderate.   150

LYDIA: Nay, I do but jest.—What's here?

Enter LUCY *in a hurry*

LUCY: O ma'am, here is Sir Anthony Absolute just come
home with your aunt.

LYDIA: They'll not come here.—Lucy, do you watch.
                                              Exit LUCY

JULIA: Yet I must go.—Sir Anthony does not know I am   155
here, and if we meet, he'll detain me, to show me the
town.—I'll take another opportunity of paying my
respects to Mrs. Malaprop, when she shall treat me, as

long as she chooses, with her select words so ingeniously
misapplied,[1] without being *mispronounced*.   160

Re-enter LUCY

LUCY: O Lud! ma'am, they are both coming up stairs.
LYDIA: Well, I'll not detain you, coz.[2]—Adieu, my dear
  Julia. I'm sure you are in haste to send to Faulkland.—
  There—through my room you'll find another stair-case.
JULIA: Adieu——[*Embrace*]   *Exit* JULIA   165
LYDIA: Here, my dear Lucy, hide these books.[3]—Quick,
  quick!—Fling *Peregrine Pickle* under the toilet—throw
  Roderick Random into the closet—put *The Innocent Adultery*
  into *The Whole Duty of Man*—thrust *Lord Aimworth* under
  the sofa—cram *Ovid* behind the bolster—there—put *The*   170
  Man of Feeling into your pocket—so, so,—now lay *Mrs.*
  Chapone in sight, and leave *Fordyce's Sermons* open on the
  table.
LUCY: O burn it, ma'am! the hair-dresser has torn away[4] as
  far as *Proper Pride*.   175
LYDIA: Never mind—open at *Sobriety*.—Fling me *Lord*
  Chesterfield's Letters.—Now for 'em.

Enter MRS. MALAPROP, *and* SIR ANTHONY ABSOLUTE

MRS. MALAPROP: There, Sir Anthony, there sits the delib-
  erate simpleton, who wants to disgrace her family, and
  lavish herself on a fellow not worth a shilling!   180
LYDIA: Madam, I thought you once——
MRS. MALAPROP: You thought, miss!—I don't know any

[1] The words are chosen carefully but used wrongly. See p. 138, for a longer note
on malapropisms.
[2] Cousin.   [3] For those named, see p. 137.
[4] In making curling-papers.

business you have to think at all.—Thought does not
become a young woman. But the point we would request
of you is, that you will promise to forget this fellow—to 185
illiterate[1] him, I say, quite from your memory.

LYDIA: Ah! madam! our memories are independent of our
wills.—It is not so easy to forget.

MRS. MALAPROP: But I say it is, miss; there is nothing on
earth so easy as to *forget*, if a person chooses to set about it. 190
—I'm sure I have as much forgot your poor dear uncle as
if he had never existed—and I thought it my duty so to do;
and let me tell you, Lydia, these violent memories don't
become a young woman.

SIR ANTHONY: Why sure she won't pretend to remember 195
what she's ordered not!—aye, this comes of her reading!

LYDIA: What crime, madam, have I committed to be treated
thus?

MRS. MALAPROP: Now don't attempt to extirpate[2] yourself
from the matter; you know I have proof controvertible[3] 200
of it.—But tell me, will you promise to do as you're bid?
—Will you take a husband of your friend's choosing?

LYDIA: Madam, I must tell you plainly, that had I no
preference for any one else, the choice you have made
would be my aversion.
205

MRS. MALAPROP: What business have you, miss, with
preference and *aversion?* They don't become a young
woman; and you ought to know, that as both always
wear off, 'tis safest in matrimony to begin with a little
aversion. I am sure I hated your poor dear uncle before 210
marriage as if he'd been a black-a-moor[4]—and yet, miss,
you are sensible what a wife I made!—and when it
pleased heav'n to release me from him, 'tis unknown
what tears I shed!—But suppose we were going to give

---

[1] Obliterate.   [2] Extricate.
[3] Incontrovertible.   [4] Negro.

you another choice, will you promise us to give up this 215
Beverley?

LYDIA: Could I belie my thoughts so far as to give that
promise, my actions would certainly as far belie my words.

MRS. MALAPROP: Take yourself to your room.—You are
fit company for nothing but your own ill-humours.   220

LYDIA: Willingly, ma'am—I cannot change for the worse.

Exit LYDIA

MRS. MALAPROP: There's a little intricate[1] hussy for you!

SIR ANTHONY: It is not to be wondered at, ma'am—all this
is the natural consequence of teaching girls to read.—Had
I a thousand daughters, by heaven! I'd as soon have them   225
taught the black art[2] as their alphabet!

MRS. MALAPROP: Nay, nay, Sir Anthony, you are an
absolute misanthropy.[3]

SIR ANTHONY: In my way hither, Mrs Malaprop, I ob-
served your niece's maid coming forth from a circulating   230
library!—She had a book in each hand—they were half-
bound volumes, with marble covers![4]—From that moment I guessed how full of duty I should see her mistress!

MRS. MALAPROP: Those are vile places, indeed!

SIR ANTHONY: Madam! a circulating library in a town is, as 235
an ever-green tree,[5] of diabolical knowledge!—It blos-
soms through the year!—And depend on it, Mrs. Malaprop, that they who are so fond of handling the leaves,
will long for the fruit at last.

MRS. MALAPROP: Fie, fie, Sir Anthony, you surely speak   240
laconically![6]

SIR ANTHONY: Why, Mrs. Malaprop, in moderation, now,
what would you have a woman know?

---

[1] Ingrate.   [2] Magic or witchcraft.   [3] Misanthropist.
[4] Spine and corners of the cover were bound in leather, and the remainder in
paper boards coloured to look like veins of marble.
[5] Cf. Genesis ii. 17: 'a tree of the knowledge of good and evil'.   [6] Ironically.

MRS. MALAPROP: Observe me,[1] Sir Anthony.—I would
by no means wish a daughter of mine to be a progeny[2] of   245
learning; I don't think so much learning becomes a young
woman; for instance—I would never let her meddle with
Greek, or Hebrew, or Algebra, or Simony, or Fluxions,
or Paradoxes,[3] or such inflammatory branches of learning
—neither would it be necessary for her to handle any of   250
your mathematical, astronomical, diabolical instruments;
—but, Sir Anthony, I would send her, at nine years old, to
a boarding-school, in order to learn a little ingenuity
and artifice.—Then, sir, she should have a supercilious[4]
knowledge in accounts;—and as she grew up, I would   255
have her instructed in geometry,[5] that she might know
something of the contagious[6] countries;—but above all,
Sir Anthony, she should be mistress of orthodoxy,[7] that
she might not mis-spell, and mis-pronounce words so
shamefully as girls usually do; and likewise that she might   260
reprehend[8] the true meaning of what she is saying.—This,
Sir Anthony, is what I would have a woman know;—and
I don't think there is a superstitious[9] article in it.

SIR ANTHONY: Well, well, Mrs. Malaprop, I will dispute
the point no further with you: though I must confess,   265
that you are a truly moderate and polite arguer, for
almost every third word you say is on my side of the
question.—But, Mrs. Malaprop, to the more important
point in debate,—you say, you have no objection to my
proposal.   270

---

[1] Mark my words.   [2] Prodigy.

[3] Simony is the buying and selling of church livings. Since she goes on to
mention 'mathematical and astronomical instruments', some vaguely scientific
suggestion is probably intended. She may have meant 'cyclometry, fluxions, and
parallax', terms referring to the measuring of cycles, the calculus, and the difference between the true and the apparent place of a planet.

[4] Superficial.   [5] Geography.   [6] Contiguous.
[7] Orthography.   [8] Apprehend.   [9] Superfluous.

MRS. MALAPROP: None, I assure you.—I am under no
positive engagement with Mr. Acres, and as Lydia is so
obstinate against him, perhaps your son may have better
success.

SIR ANTHONY: Well, madam, I will write for the boy 275
directly.—He knows not a syllable of this yet, though
I have for some time had the proposal in my head. He is at
present with his regiment.

MRS. MALAPROP: We have never seen your son, Sir
Anthony; but I hope no objection on his side.   280

SIR ANTHONY: Objection!—let him object if he dare!—
No, no, Mrs. Malaprop, Jack knows that the least demur
puts me in a frenzy directly.—My process was always
very simple—in their younger days, 'twas 'Jack do this';—
if he demurred—I knocked him down—and if he grum- 285
bled at that—I always sent him out of the room.

MRS. MALAPROP: Aye, and the properest way, o' my conscience!—nothing is so conciliating[1] to young people as
severity.—Well, Sir Anthony, I shall give Mr. Acres his
discharge, and prepare Lydia to receive your son's invoca- 290
tions;[2]—and I hope you will represent *her* to the Captain
as an object not altogether illegible.[3]

SIR ANTHONY: Madam, I will handle the subject prudently.
—Well, I must leave you—and let me beg you, Mrs.
Malaprop, to enforce this matter roundly to the girl;— 295
—take my advice—keep a tight hand—if she rejects this
proposal—clap her under lock and key:—and if you were
just to let the servants forget to bring her dinner for three
or four days, you can't conceive how she'd come about!
                                        Exit SIR ANTHONY

MRS. MALAPROP: Well, at any rate I shall be glad to get her 300
from under my intuition.[4]—She has somehow discovered

---

[1] Constricting   [2] A possible usage, but she may mean 'protestations'.
[3] Eligible.   [4] Tuition.

my partiality for Sir Lucius O'Trigger—sure, Lucy can't
have betrayed me!—No, the girl is such a simpleton, I
should have made her confess it.—Lucy!—Lucy!—[*Calls*].
Had she been one of your artificial ones,[1] I should never   305
have trusted her.

Enter LUCY

LUCY: Did you call, ma'am?

MRS. MALAPROP: Yes, girl.—Did you see Sir Lucius while
you was[2] out?

LUCY: No, indeed, ma'am, not a glimpse of him.   310

MRS. MALAPROP: You are sure, Lucy, that you never
mentioned——

LUCY: O Gemini![3] I'd sooner cut my tongue out.

MRS. MALAPROP: Well, don't let your simplicity be imposed on.   315

LUCY: No, ma'am.

MRS. MALAPROP: So, come to me presently, and I'll give
you another letter to Sir Lucius;—but mind Lucy—if
ever you betray what you are intrusted with—(unless it
be other people's secrets to me) you forfeit my malevol-   320
ence[4] for ever:—and your being a simpleton shall be no
excuse for your locality.[5]   *Exit* MRS. MALAPROP

LUCY: Ha! ha! ha!—So, my dear *simplicity*, let me give you
a little respite—[*altering her manner*]—let girls in my
station be as fond as they please of appearing expert, and   325
knowing in their trusts;—commend me to a mask of
silliness, and a pair of sharp eyes for my own interest under
it!—Let me see to what account have I turned my
simplicity lately—[*looks at a paper*]. For *abetting Miss Lydia*

---

[1] Artful.   [2] A common usage of the day.
[3] Possibly a corruption of 'Jesu domine'. Gemini, the twins, is a sign of the
Zodiac, and a constellation.   [4] Benevolence.   [5] Loquacity.

Languish in a design of running away with an Ensign!—in   330
money—sundry times—twelve pound twelve—gowns, five—
hats, ruffles, caps, &c., &c.,—numberless!—From the said
Ensign, within this last month, six guineas and a half.—About
a quarter's pay!—Item, *from Mrs. Malaprop, for betraying*
the young people to her—when I found matters were likely   335
to be discovered—*two guineas, and a black paduasoy.*[1]—
Item, *from Mr. Acres, for carrying divers letters*—which I
never delivered—*two guineas, and a pair of buckles.*—Item,
from Sir Lucius O' Trigger—three crowns—two gold pocket-
pieces[2]—*and a silver snuff-box!*—Well done, *simplicity!*—   340
Yet I was forced to make my Hibernian[3] believe, that he
was corresponding, not with the *aunt*, but with the *niece*;
for, though not over rich, I found he had too much pride
and delicacy to sacrifice the feelings of a gentleman to the
necessities of his fortune.   *Exit*   345

[1] A corded silk gown.   [2] Coins carried as lucky charms.   [3] Irishman.

Act II scene i

FAG: Sir, while I was there Sir Anthony came in: I told him, you had sent me to inquire after his health, and to know if he was at leisure to see you.

ABSOLUTE: And what did he say on hearing I was at Bath?

FAG: Sir, in my life I never saw an elderly gentleman more 5 astonished! He started back two or three paces, rapped out a dozen interjectoral[1] oaths, and asked, what the devil had brought you here!

ABSOLUTE: Well, sir, and what did you say?

FAG: O, I lied, sir—I forget the precise lie, but you may 10 depend on't, he got no truth from me. Yet, with submission, for fear of blunders in future, I should be glad to fix what *has* brought us to Bath: in order that we may lie a little consistently.—Sir Anthony's servants were curious, sir, very curious indeed. 15

ABSOLUTE: You have said nothing to them——?

FAG: O, not a word, sir—not a word.—Mr. Thomas, indeed, the coachman (whom I take to be the discreetest of whips)——

ABSOLUTE: 'Sdeath![2]—you rascal! you have not trusted 20 him!

FAG: O, *no*, sir!—no—no—not a syllable, upon my veracity! —He was, indeed, a little inquisitive; but I was sly, sir—

[1] Interjectional.　　　　[2] An oath, from 'God's death'.

devilish sly!—My master (said I), honest Thomas (you
know, sir, one says *honest* to one's inferiors) is come to   25
Bath to *recruit*—Yes, sir—I said, to *recruit*—and whether
for men, money, or constitution,[1] you know, sir, is
nothing to him, nor any one else.

ABSOLUTE: Well—*recruit*—will do—let it be so——

FAG: O, sir, recruit will do surprisingly—indeed, to give the   30
thing an air; I told Thomas, that your Honour had already
enlisted five disbanded chairmen,[2] seven minority waiters,[3]
and thirteen billiard markers.[4]

ABSOLUTE: You blockhead, never say more than is
necessary.   35

FAG: I beg pardon, sir—I beg pardon—But with submission,
a lie is nothing unless one supports it.—Sir, whenever I
draw on my invention for a good current lie, I always
forge indorsements, as well as the bill.

ABSOLUTE: Well, take care you don't hurt your credit, by   40
offering too much security.[5]—Is Mr. Faulkland returned?

FAG: He is above, sir, changing his dress.

ABSOLUTE: Can you tell whether he has been informed of
Sir Anthony's and Miss Melville's arrival?

FAG: I fancy not, sir; he has seen no one since he came in,   45
but his gentleman, who was with him at Bristol.—I think,
sir, I hear Mr. Faulkland coming down—

[1] Strength.

[2] The Sedan chair was made to carry one person, and was borne by two
chairmen, who stood in the shafts at each end.

[3] A crux. A possible meaning is that of youthful or part-time waiters. Philip B.
Daghlian (in *Mod. Lang. Quart.*, vi (1945), 421–2) suggests that it alludes to Robert
Mackreth, once billiard-marker and waiter at Arthur's coffee house, but M.P. for
Castle Rising from 1774.

[4] Men who kept the score in billiard rooms.

[5] The play on words concerns crediting what Fag says and his obtaining financial
credit. In making out a bill of exchange, Fag will ask a paying agent (here, his
invention) to hand over something to the payee at some future date. If the payee
requires the sum immediately, he may sell the bill to someone else by endorsing it,
so becoming security for payment.

ABSOLUTE: Go, tell him, I am here.

FAG: Yes, sir—*[going]*. I beg pardon, sir, but should Sir
Anthony call, you will do me the favour to remember, that   50
we are *recruiting*, if you please.

ABSOLUTE: Well, well.

FAG: And in tenderness to my character, if your Honour
could bring in the chairmen and waiters, I shall esteem
it as an obligation;—for though I never scruple a lie to   55
serve my master, yet it hurts one's conscience to be found
out.   *Exit*

ABSOLUTE: Now for my whimsical friend—if he does not
know that his mistress is here, I'll tease him a little before
I tell him——   60

Enter FAULKLAND

Faulkland, you're welcome to Bath again; you are punctual
in your return.

FAULKLAND: Yes; I had nothing to detain me, when I had
finished the business I went on. Well, what news since I
left you? How stand matters between you and   65
Lydia?

ABSOLUTE: Faith, much as they were; I have not seen her
since our quarrel, however I expect to be recalled every
hour.

FAULKLAND: Why don't you persuade her to go off with   70
you at once?

ABSOLUTE: What, and lose two thirds of her fortune? You
forget that my friend.—No, no, I could have brought her
to that long ago.

FAULKLAND: Nay then, you trifle too long—if you are sure   75
of *her*, propose to the aunt *in your own character*, and write
to Sir Anthony for his consent.

ABSOLUTE: Softly, softly, for though I am convinced my

little Lydia would elope with me as Ensign Beverley, yet
am I by no means certain that she would take me with the   80
impediment of our friends' consent, a regular humdrum
wedding, and the reversion[1] of a good fortune on my side;
no, no, I must prepare her gradually for the discovery,
and make myself necessary to her, before I risk it.—Well,
but Faulkland, you'll dine with us to-day at the hotel?   85

FAULKLAND: Indeed I cannot: I am not in spirits to be of
such a party.

ABSOLUTE: By heavens! I shall forswear your company.
You are the most teasing, captious, incorrigible lover!—
Do love like a man!   90

FAULKLAND: I own I am unfit for company.

ABSOLUTE: Am not *I* a lover; aye, and a romantic one too?
Yet do I carry everywhere with me such a confounded
farrago[2] of doubts, fears, hopes, wishes, and all the
flimsy furniture of a country miss's brain!   95

FAULKLAND: Ah! Jack, your heart and soul are not, like
mine, fixed immutably on one only object.—You throw
for a large stake, but losing—you could stake, and throw
again:—but I have set my sum of happiness on this cast,
and not to succeed were to be stripped of all.   100

ABSOLUTE: But, for heaven's sake! what grounds for apprehension can your whimsical brain conjure up at
present?

FAULKLAND: What grounds for apprehension did you say?
Heavens! are there not a thousand! I fear for her spirits—   105
her health—her life.—My absence may fret her; her
anxiety for my return, her fears for me, may oppress her
gentle temper. And for her health—does not every hour
bring me cause to be alarmed? If it rains, some shower
may even then have chilled her delicate frame!—If the   110
wind be keen, some rude blast may have affected her!

---

[1] Inheritance of an estate.   [2] Confused mixture.

The heat of noon, the dews of the evening, may endanger the life of her, for whom only I value mine. O! Jack, when delicate and feeling souls are separated, there is not a feature in the sky, not a movement of the elements, not an aspiration[1] of the breeze, but hints some cause for a lover's apprehension! 115

ABSOLUTE: Aye, but we may choose whether we will take the hint or not.—So then, Faulkland, if you were convinced that Julia were well and in spirits, you would be entirely content? 120

FAULKLAND: I should be happy beyond measure—I am anxious only for that.

ABSOLUTE: Then to cure your anxiety at once—Miss Melville is in perfect health, and is at this moment in Bath! 125

FAULKLAND: Nay, Jack—don't trifle with me.

ABSOLUTE: She is arrived here with my father within this hour.

FAULKLAND: Can you be serious? 130

ABSOLUTE: I thought you knew Sir Anthony better than to be surprised at a sudden whim of this kind.—Seriously then, it is as I tell you—upon my honour.

FAULKLAND: My dear friend!—Hollo, Du-Peigne! My hat—my dear Jack—now nothing on earth can give me a moment's uneasiness. 135

Enter FAG

FAG: Sir, Mr. Acres just arrived is below.

ABSOLUTE: Stay, Faulkland, this Acres lives within a mile of Sir Anthony, and he shall tell you how your mistress has been ever since you left her.—Fag, show the gentleman up. 140   *Exit* FAG

---

[1] Breath.

FAULKLAND: What, is he much acquainted in the family?

ABSOLUTE: O, very intimate: I insist on your not going: besides, his character will divert you.

FAULKLAND: Well, I should like to ask him a few questions. 145

ABSOLUTE: He is likewise a rival of mine—that is of my *other self's*, for he does not think his friend Capt. Absolute ever saw the lady in question;—and it is ridiculous enough to hear him complain to me of *one Beverley*, a concealed skulking rival, who—— 150

FAULKLAND: Hush!—He's here.

Enter ACRES

ACRES: Hah! my dear friend, noble captain, and honest Jack, how do'st thou? Just arrived faith, as you see.—Sir, your humble servant. Warm work on the roads Jack— Odds whips and wheels![1] I've travelled like a comet, with 155 a tail of dust all the way as long as the Mall.[2]

ABSOLUTE: Ah! Bob, you are indeed an eccentric planet, but we know your attraction hither—Give me leave to introduce Mr. Faulkland to you; Mr. Faulkland, Mr. Acres. 160

ACRES: Sir, I am most heartily glad to see you: sir, I solicit your connections.[3]—Hey Jack—what this is Mr. Faulkland, who——?

ABSOLUTE: Aye, Bob, Miss Melville's Mr. Faulkland.

ACRES: Od'so! she and your father can be but just arrived 165 before me—I suppose you have seen them.—Ah! Mr. Faulkland, you are indeed a happy man.

FAULKLAND: I have not seen Miss Melville yet, sir—I hope she enjoyed full health and spirits in Devonshire?

ACRES: Never knew her better in my life, sir—never better. 170

[1] One of Acres's 'oaths referential': see his speech, p. 57.
[2] The fashionable walk to the north of St. James's Park.
[3] Beg leave to become acquainted with you.

—Odd's blushes and blooms! she has been as healthy as the German Spa.[1]

FAULKLAND: Indeed!—I did hear that she had been a little indisposed.

ACRES: False, false, sir—only said to vex you: quite the reverse I assure you.

FAULKLAND: There, Jack, you see she has the advantage of me; I had almost fretted myself ill.

ABSOLUTE: Now are you angry with your mistress for not having been sick.

FAULKLAND: No, no, you misunderstand me:—yet surely a little trifling indisposition is not an unnatural consequence of absence from those we love.—Now confess—isn't there something unkind in this violent, robust, unfeeling health?

ABSOLUTE: O, it was very unkind of her to be well in your absence, to be sure!

ACRES: Good apartments, Jack.

FAULKLAND: Well, sir, but you were saying that Miss Melville has been so *exceedingly* well—what, then she has been merry and gay I suppose?—Always in spirits—hey?

ACRES: Merry! Odds crickets! she has been the belle and spirit of the company wherever she has been—so lively and entertaining! so full of wit and humour!

FAULKLAND: There, Jack, there—O, by my soul! there is an innate levity in woman, that nothing can overcome. —What! happy, and I away!

ABSOLUTE: Have done:—how foolish this is! Just now you were only apprehensive for your mistress's *spirits*.

FAULKLAND: Why, Jack, have I been the joy and spirit of the company?

ABSOLUTE: No, indeed, you have not.

---

[1] A health resort near the German border of Belgium, and celebrated for its mineral springs.

FAULKLAND: Have I been lively and entertaining?

ABSOLUTE: O, upon my word, I acquit you.

FAULKLAND: Have I been full of wit and humour?   205

ABSOLUTE: No, faith, to do you justice, you have been confoundedly stupid indeed.

ACRES: What's the matter with the gentleman?

ABSOLUTE: He is only expressing his great satisfaction at hearing that Julia has been so well and happy—that's all— 210 hey, Faulkland?

FAULKLAND: Oh! I am rejoiced to hear it—yes, yes, she has a *happy* disposition!

ACRES: That she has indeed—then she is so accomplished—so sweet a voice—so expert at her harpsichord—such a 215 mistress of flat and sharp, squallante, rumblante, and quiverante![1]—there was this time month—Odds min- nums[2] and crotchets! how she did chirrup at Mrs. Piano's[3] concert!

FAULKLAND: There again, what say you to this? You see 220 she has been all mirth and song—not a thought of me!

ABSOLUTE: Pho! man, is not music the food of love?[4]

FAULKLAND: Well, well, it may be so.—Pray Mr.—— what's his d——d name? Do you remember what songs 225 Miss Melville sung?

ACRES: Not I, indeed.

ABSOLUTE: Stay now, they were some pretty, melancholy, purling stream airs,[5] I warrant; perhaps you may recollect: —did she sing—'*When absent from my soul's delight*'?[6]   230

ACRES: No, that wa'n't it.

[1] Acres tries to give an Italian air to the English words 'squalling', 'rumbling', and 'quivering'

[2] Minims are half the value of a semibreve, and crotchets, a quarter.

[3] The musical direction for 'soft' or 'softly'.

[4] Cf. the first line of *Twelfth Night*: 'If music be the food of love, play on.'

[5] Gently pleasing, rippling sounds.   [6] See the note on the songs on p. 139.

ABSOLUTE: Or—'*Go, gentle gales*'?[1]——'*Go, gentle gales!*'
[*Sings*]

ACRES: O no! nothing like it.—Odds! now I recollect one of them—'*My heart's my own, my will is free.*'[2]   [*Sings*]   235

FAULKLAND: Fool! fool that I am! to fix all my happiness on such a trifler! 'Sdeath! to make herself the pipe and ballad-monger of a circle! to soothe her light heart with catches[3] and glees![4]—What can you say to this, sir?   240

ABSOLUTE: Why, that I should be glad to hear my mistress had been so merry, *sir*.

FAULKLAND: Nay, nay, nay—I am not sorry that she has been happy—no, no, I am glad of that—I would not have had her sad or sick—yet surely a sympathetic heart would   245
have shown itself even in the choice of a song—she might have been temperately healthy, and, somehow, plaintively gay;—but she has been dancing too, I doubt not!

ACRES: What does the gentleman say about dancing?

ABSOLUTE: He says the lady we speak of dances as well as   250
she sings.

ACRES: Aye truly, does she—there was at our last race-ball——

FAULKLAND: Hell and the devil! There! there!—I told you so! I told you so! Oh! she thrives in my absence!—Dan-   255
cing!—but her whole feelings have been in opposition with mine!—I have been anxious, silent, pensive, sedentary—my days have been hours of care, my nights of watchfulness.—She has been all Health! Spirit! Laugh! Song! Dance!—Oh! d—n'd, d—n'd levity!   260

ABSOLUTE: For heaven's sake! Faulkland, don't expose yourself so.—Suppose she has danced, what then?— does not the ceremony of society often oblige——

---

[1] See the note on the songs on p. 139.
[2] See p. 140.
[3] Short, amusing songs.
[4] Unaccompanied part-songs.

FAULKLAND: Well, well, I'll contain myself—perhaps as
you say—for form sake.—What, Mr. Acres, you were 265
praising Miss Melville's manner of dancing a *minuet*—
hey?

ACRES: O I dare insure her for that—but what I was going
to speak of was her *country dancing:*—Odds swimmings!
she has such an air with her!—   270

FAULKLAND: Now disappointment on her!—defend this,
Absolute, why don't you defend this?—Country-dances!
jigs, and reels! Am I to blame now? A minuet I could
have forgiven—I should not have minded that—I say I
should not have regarded a minuet—but *country-dances!* 275
Z——ds! had she made one in a cotillion[1]—I believe I
could have forgiven even that—but to be monkey-led for
a night!—to run the gauntlet thro' a string of amorous
palming puppies![2]—to show paces like a managed[3] filly!
—O Jack, there never can be but *one* man in the 280
world, whom a truly modest and delicate woman
ought to pair with in a *country-dance*; and even then,
the rest of the couples should be her great uncles and
aunts!

ABSOLUTE: Aye, to be sure!—grand-fathers and grand- 285
mothers!

FAULKLAND: If there be but one vicious mind in the set,[4]
'twill spread like a contagion—the action of their pulse
beats to the lascivious movement of the jig—their
quivering, warm-breathed sighs impregnate the very air— 290

[1] The minuet was a dignified dance performed in small steps, the cotillion was
livelier, and country dances were boisterous. The distinctions were brought out
in the *General Evening Post*, 3–5 June 1777, in a report on a ball at court: 'about a
dozen minuets were danced, and then the company rose to country dances and
cotillons'.

[2] Raw, conceited fellows, anxious to get their hands on the girls.

[3] Taught the 'manège', stepping and moving according to the strict practice of
the riding school.

[4] The number of people required for the figure of a dance.

the atmosphere becomes electrical[1] to love, and each amorous spark darts thro'every link of the chain!—I must leave you—I own I am somewhat flurried—and that confounded looby[2] has perceived it.   [*Going*]

ABSOLUTE: Nay, but stay, Faulkland, and thank Mr. Acres   295
for his good news.

FAULKLAND: D—n his news!   *Exit* FAULKLAND

ABSOLUTE: Ha! ha! ha! Poor Faulkland! five minutes since
—'nothing on earth could give him a moment's uneasiness!'   300

ACRES: The gentleman wa'n't angry at my praising his
mistress, was he?

ABSOLUTE: A little jealous, I believe, Bob.

ACRES: You don't say so? Ha! ha! jealous of me?—that's a
good joke.   305

ABSOLUTE: There's nothing strange in that, Bob; let me
tell you, that sprightly grace and insinuating manner of
yours will do some mischief among the girls here.

ACRES: Ah! you joke—ha! ha!—mischief—ha! ha! But you
know I am not my own property, my dear Lydia has   310
forestalled me.—She could never abide me in the country,
because I used to dress so badly—but odds frogs[3] and
tambours![4] I shan't take matters so here—now ancient
madam[5] has no voice in it.—I'll make my old clothes
know who's master—I shall straightway cashier[6] the hunt-   315
ing-frock—and render my leather breeches incapable.[7]—
My hair has been in training some time.

ABSOLUTE: Indeed!

---

[1] 'These exhalations, or subtile effluvia, constitute electricity. . . . They seem to adhere to the extremities of the bodies which they surround, and from which they recede, in the form of sparks' (*A New and Complete Dictionary of Arts and Sciences* (2nd ed., 1763) p. 1050).   [2] Fool.

[3] Ornamental loop or tuft on a military tunic.

[4] Round frame used in embroidering.   [5] His mother: 'the old lady'.

[6] Dismiss from service.   [7] Unable to give further service.

ACRES: Aye—and tho'ff the side-curls are a little restive, my
hind-part takes to it very kindly.   320

ABSOLUTE: O, you'll polish, I doubt not.

ACRES: Absolutely I propose so.—Then if I can find out this
Ensign Beverley, odds triggers and flints![1] I'll make him
know the difference o't.

ABSOLUTE: Spoke like a man—but pray, Bob, I observe you   325
have got an odd kind of a new method of swearing——

ACRES: Ha! ha! you've taken notice of it—'tis genteel, isn't
it?—I didn't invent it myself, though; but a commander
in our militia[2]—a great scholar, I assure you—says that
there is no meaning in the common oaths, and that   330
nothing but their antiquity makes them respectable;—
because, he says, the ancients would never stick to an oath
or two, but would say, by Jove! or by Bacchus! or by
Mars! or by Venus! or by Pallas! according to the senti-
ment[3]—so that to swear with propriety, says my little   335
major, the 'oath should be an echo to the sense';[4] and this
we call the *oath referential*, or *sentimental swearing*—ha! ha!
ha! 'tis genteel,[5] isn't it?

ABSOLUTE: Very genteel,[6] and very new indeed—and I
dare say will supplant all other figures of imprecation.   340

ACRES: Aye, aye, the best terms will grow obsolete—Damns
have had their day.

Enter FAG

FAG: Sir, there is a gentleman below, desires to see you.—
Shall I show him into the parlour?

[1] The trigger of a gun released the hammer which, striking the flint, produced
a spark to ignite the powder.

[2] Trained bands who armed themselves, for their own defence. They were under
the command of the Lords-lieutenants.   [3] The opinion expressed.

[4] Pope, *An Essay in Criticism* (1711), lines 364–5:
　　　'Tis not enough no harshness gives offence,
　　　The sound must seem an echo to the sense.'

[5] Suited to a gentleman.   [6] Affected.

ABSOLUTE: Aye—you may.   345

ACRES: Well, I must be gone——

ABSOLUTE: Stay; who is it, Fag?

FAG: Your father, sir.

ABSOLUTE: You puppy, why didn't you show him up
    directly?   *Exit* FAG   350

ACRES: You have business with Sir Anthony.—I expect a
    message from Mrs. Malaprop at my lodgings—I have
    sent also to my dear friend, Sir Lucius O'Trigger.—Adieu,
    Jack, we must meet at night, when you shall give me a
    dozen bumpers[1] to little Lydia.   355

ABSOLUTE: That I will, with all my heart.   *Exit* ACRES

ABSOLUTE: Now for a parental lecture.—I hope he has
    heard nothing of the business that has brought me here
    —I wish the gout[2] had held him fast in Devonshire, with
    all my soul!   360

Enter SIR ANTHONY

ABSOLUTE: Sir, I am delighted to see you here; and looking
    so well!—Your sudden arrival at Bath made me appre-
    hensive for your health.

SIR ANTHONY: Very apprehensive, I dare say, Jack.—What
    you are recruiting here, hey?   365

ABSOLUTE: Yes, sir, I am on duty.

SIR ANTHONY: Well, Jack, I am glad to see you, tho' I did
    not expect it, for I was going to write to you on a little
    matter of business.—Jack, I have been considering that I
    grow old and infirm, and shall probably not trouble you   370
    long.

ABSOLUTE: Pardon me, sir, I never saw you look more
    strong and hearty; and I pray frequently that you may
    continue so.

[1] You shall drink to her, with full glass, a dozen times.
[2] Painful swellings of the joints, common among the leisured classes.

SIR ANTHONY: I hope your prayers may be heard with all 375
my heart. Well then, Jack, I have been considering that I
am so strong and hearty, I may continue to plague you a
long time.—Now, Jack, I am sensible that the income of
your commission[1] and what I have hitherto allowed
you, is but a small pittance for a lad of your spirit. 380

ABSOLUTE: Sir, you are very good.

SIR ANTHONY: And it is my wish, while yet I live, to have
my boy make some figure in the world.—I have resolved,
therefore, to fix you at once in a noble independence.

ABSOLUTE: Sir, your kindness overpowers me—such 385
generosity makes the gratitude of reason more lively than
the sensations even of filial affection.

SIR ANTHONY: I am glad you are so sensible of my attention—and you shall be master of a large estate in a few
weeks. 390

ABSOLUTE: Let my future life, sir, speak my gratitude: I
cannot express the sense I have of your munificence.——
Yet, sir, I presume you would not wish me to quit the
army?

SIR ANTHONY: O, that shall be as your wife chooses. 395

ABSOLUTE: My wife, sir!

SIR ANTHONY: Aye, aye,—settle that between you—settle
that between you.

ABSOLUTE: A *wife*, sir, did you say?

SIR ANTHONY: Aye, a wife—why; did not I mention her 400
before?

ABSOLUTE: Not a word of her, sir.

SIR ANTHONY: Odd so!—I mus'nt' forget *her*, tho'.—Yes,
Jack, the independence I was talking of is by a marriage—

[1] His warrant as an ensign. *The Royal Kalendar* (1793), p. 141, notes that an
ensign in the Foot Guards drew 5s. 10d. a day and 4s. 6d. subsistence, while a
second lieutenant in a Foot Regiment drew 3s. 8d. and 3s. 0d. These rates were full
pay

the fortune is saddled with a wife—but I suppose that 405
makes no difference.

ABSOLUTE: Sir! sir!—you amaze me!

SIR ANTHONY: Why, what the devil's the matter with the
fool? Just now you were all gratitude and duty.

ABSOLUTE: I was, sir,—you talked to me of independence 410
and a fortune, but not a word of a wife.

SIR ANTHONY: Why—what difference does that make?
Odds life, sir! if you have the estate, you must take it with
the live stock[1] on it, as it stands.

ABSOLUTE: If my happiness is to be the price, I must beg 415
leave to decline the purchase.—Pray, sir, who is the
lady?

SIR ANTHONY: What's that to you, sir?—Come, give me
your promise to love, and to marry her directly.

ABSOLUTE: Sure, sir, this is not very reasonable, to summon 420
my affections for a lady I know nothing of!

SIR ANTHONY: I am sure, sir, 'tis more unreasonable in you
to *object* to a lady you know nothing of.

ABSOLUTE: Then, sir, I must tell you plainly, that my inclinations are fixed on another—my heart is engaged to an 425
angel.

SIR ANTHONY: Then pray let it send an excuse.——It is
very sorry—but *business* prevents its waiting on her.

ABSOLUTE: But my vows are pledged to her.

SIR ANTHONY: Let her foreclose, Jack; let her foreclose; they 430
are not worth redeeming:[2] besides, you have the angel's
vows in exchange, I suppose; so there can be no loss there.

ABSOLUTE: You must excuse me, sir, if I tell you, once for
all, that in this point I cannot obey you.

---

[1] Living creatures: as opposed to 'dead stock', furniture and equipment.

[2] A 'pledge' was a security given for something borrowed, and when it was not
redeemed within the stated time, the lender could regard the security as his own
property.

SIR ANTHONY: Harkee', Jack;—I have heard you for some 435
time with patience—I have been cool—quite cool; but
take care—you know I am compliance itself—when I am
not thwarted;—no one more easily led—when I have my
own way;—but don't put me in a frenzy.

ABSOLUTE: Sir, I must repeat it—in this I cannot obey you. 440

SIR ANTHONY: Now, d—n me! if ever I call you *Jack* again
while I live!

ABSOLUTE: Nay, sir, but hear me.

SIR ANTHONY: Sir, I won't hear a word—not a word!
not one word! so give me your promise by a nod—and 445
I'll tell you what, Jack—I mean, you dog—if you don't,
by——

ABSOLUTE: What, sir, promise to link myself to some mass
of ugliness! to ——

SIR ANTHONY: Z——ds! sirrah! the lady shall be as ugly as 450
I choose: she shall have a hump on each shoulder; she
shall be as crooked as the Crescent; her one eye shall roll
like the Bull's in Cox's Museum[1]—she shall have a skin
like a mummy, and the beard of a Jew—she shall be all
this, sirrah!—yet I'll make you ogle her all day, and sit up 455
all night to write sonnets on her beauty.

ABSOLUTE: This is reason and moderation indeed!

SIR ANTHONY: None of your sneering, puppy! no grin-
ning, jackanapes![2]

ABSOLUTE: Indeed, sir, I never was in a worse humour for 460
mirth in my life.

SIR ANTHONY: 'Tis false, sir! I know you are laughing in
your sleeve: I know you'll grin when I am gone, sirrah!

ABSOLUTE: Sir, I hope I know my duty better.

SIR ANTHONY: None of your passion, sir! none of your 465

---

[1] James Cox was a jeweller who exhibited mechanical 'toys' in Spring Gardens,
1772–75. One of them was 'a curious bull' and another was 'a pedestal of four bulls'.
[2] Impertinent youngster.

violence! if you please.—It won't do with me, I promise
you.

ABSOLUTE: Indeed, sir, I never was cooler in my life.

SIR ANTHONY: 'Tis a confounded lie!—I know you are in
a passion in your heart; I know you are, you hypocritical   470
young dog! But it won't do.

ABSOLUTE: Nay, sir, upon my word.

SIR ANTHONY: So you will fly out! can't you be cool, like
me? What the devil good can *passion* do!—*Passion* is of no
service, you impudent, insolent, over-bearing reprobate!   475
—There you sneer again!—don't provoke me!—but you
rely upon the mildness of my temper—you do, you dog!
you play upon the meekness of my disposition! Yet take
care—the patience of a saint may be overcome at last!—
but mark! I give you six hours and a half to consider of   480
this: if you then agree, without any condition, to do
everything on earth that I choose, why—confound you!
I may in time forgive you——If not, z——ds! don't enter
the same hemisphere with me! don't dare to breathe the
same air, or use the same light with me; but get an atmo-   485
sphere and a sun of your own! I'll strip you of your commission; I'll lodge a five-and-threepence[1] in the hands of
trustees, and you shall live on the interest.—I'll disown
you, I'll disinherit you, I'll unget you! and—d—n me, if
ever I call you Jack again!   *Exit* SIR ANTHONY   490

ABSOLUTE *solus*

ABSOLUTE: Mild, gentle, considerate father—I kiss your
hands.—What a tender method of giving his opinion in
these matters Sir Anthony has! I dare not trust him with
the truth.—I wonder what old, wealthy hag it is that he
wants to bestow on me!—yet he married himself for love!   495

---

[1] Cut him off with a quarter of a guinea.

and was in his youth a bold intriguer, and a gay companion!

Enter FAG

FAG: Assuredly, sir, our father is wrath to a degree; he comes
down stairs eight or ten steps at a time—muttering,
growling, and thumping the bannisters all the way: I, and 500
the cook's dog, stand bowing at the door—rap! he gives
me a stroke on the head with his cane; bids me carry that
to my master; then kicking the poor turnspit[1] into the
area, d—ns us all for a puppy triumvirate![2]—Upon my
credit, sir, were I in your place, and found my father such 505
very bad company, I should certainly drop his acquaintance.

ABSOLUTE: Cease your impertinence, sir, at present.—Did
you come in for nothing more?—Stand out of the way!
Pushes him aside, and exit

FAG *solus*

FAG: Soh! Sir Anthony trims[3] my master. He is afraid to 510
reply to his father—then vents his spleen on poor Fag!—
When one is vexed by one person, to revenge one's self on
another, who happens to come in the way—is the
vilest injustice! Ah! it shows the worst temper—the
basest—— 515

Enter ERRAND-BOY

BOY: Mr. Fag! Mr. Fag! your master calls you.
FAG: Well, you little, dirty puppy, you need not bawl so!—
The meanest disposition! the——
BOY: Quick, quick, Mr. Fag.

---

[1] Roasting spits were turned by small dogs pressing on a treadwheel.
[2] Impertinent trio.   [3] Scolds.

FAG: Quick! quick! you impudent jackanapes! am I to be   520
commanded by you too? you little, impertinent, insolent,
kitchen-bred——   *Exit, kicking and beating him*

Scene ii

The North Parade

Enter LUCY

LUCY: So—I shall have another rival to add to my mistress's
list—Captain Absolute.——However, I shall not enter his
name till my purse has received notice in form.[1] Poor
Acres is dismissed!—Well, I have done him a last friendly
office, in letting him know that Beverley was here before   5
him.—Sir Lucius is generally more punctual when he expects to hear from his *dear Dalia*, as he calls her:—I wonder
he's not here!—I have a little scruple of conscience from
this deceit; tho' I should not be paid so well, if my hero
knew that *Delia* was near fifty, and her own mistress.   10

Enter SIR LUCIUS O'TRIGGER

SIR LUCIUS: Hah! my little embassadress—upon my conscience I have been looking for you; I have been on the
South Parade this half-hour.
LUCY: [*speaking simply*]: O gemini! and I have been waiting
for your worship here on the North.   15
SIR LUCIUS: Faith!—may be that was the reason we did not
meet; and it is very comical too, how you could go out
and I not see you—for I was only taking a nap at the

[1] A bribe.

Parade Coffee-house, and I chose the *window* on purpose
that I might not miss you.   20

LUCY: My stars! Now I'd wager a sixpence I went by while
you were asleep.

SIR LUCIUS: Sure enough it must have been so—and I never
dreamt it was so late, till I waked. Well, but my little girl,
have you got nothing for me?   25

LUCY: Yes, but I have—I've got a letter for you in my
pocket.

SIR LUCIUS: O faith! I guessed you weren't come empty-
handed—well—let me see what the dear creature says.

LUCY: There, Sir Lucius.   [*Gives him a letter*] 30

SIR LUCIUS: [*reads*]: '*Sir—there is often a sudden incentive*[1]
impulse in love, that has a greater induction[2] *than years of
domestic combination: such was the commotion I felt at the first
superfluous*[3] *view of Sir Lucius O' Trigger.*'—Very pretty,
upon my word. '*Female punctuation*[4] *forbids me to say*   35
more; yet let me add, that it will give me joy infallible[5] *to find
Sir Lucius worthy the last criterion of my affections.*—DELIA.'
Upon my conscience! Lucy, your lady is a great mistress of language.—Faith, she's quite the queen of the
dictionary!—for the devil a word dare refuse coming at   40
her call—though one would think it was quite out of
hearing.

LUCY: Aye, sir, a lady of her experience——

SIR LUCIUS: Experience! what, at seventeen?

LUCY: O true, sir—but then she reads so—my stars! how   45
she will read off-hand!

SIR LUCIUS: Faith, she must be very deep read to write this
way—though she is rather an arbitrary writer too—for
here are a great many poor words pressed[6] into the service

---

[1] Instinctive.   [2] Production.   [3] Superficial.
[4] Punctilio.   [5] Ineffable.
[6] 'Impressed': forced by Press Gang into the service of army or navy.

of this note, that would get their *habeas corpus*[1] from any   50
court in Christendom.

LUCY: Ah! Sir Lucius, if you were to hear how she talks of you!

SIR LUCIUS: O tell her, I'll make her the best husband in the
world, and Lady O'Trigger into the bargain!—But we
must get the old gentlewoman's consent—and do every-   55
thing fairly.

LUCY: Nay, Sir Lucius, I thought you wa'n't rich enough
to be so nice.[2]

SIR LUCIUS: Upon my word, young woman, you have hit
it:—I am so poor that I can't afford to do a dirty action.—   60
If I did not want money I'd steal your mistress and her
fortune with a great deal of pleasure.—However, my
pretty girl [*gives her money*], here's a little something to
buy you a ribband; and meet me in the evening, and I'll
give you an answer to this. So, hussy, take a kiss before-   65
hand, to put you in mind.   [*Kisses her*]

LUCY: O lud! Sir Lucius—I never seed such a gemman! My
lady won't like you if you're so impudent.

SIR LUCIUS: Faith she will, Lucy——that same——pho!
what's the name of it?—*Modesty!*——is a quality in a lover   70
more praised by the women than liked; so, if your
mistress asks you whether Sir Lucius ever gave you a kiss,
tell her fifty—my dear.

LUCY: What, would you have me tell her a lie?

SIR LUCIUS: Ah, then, you baggage![3] I'll make it a truth   75
presently.

LUCY: For shame now; here is some one coming.

SIR LUCIUS: O faith, I'll quiet your conscience.

Sees FAG.—*Exit, humming a tune*

---

[1] A writ of *habeas corpus* ('You may have the body') requires that a detainee
should be taken before a judge so that the legality of the arrest may be considered.
The sense, here, is 'release'.

[2] Scrupulous.   [3] A saucy girl.

Enter FAG

FAG: So, so ma'am. I humbly beg pardon.

LUCY: O lud!—now, Mr. Fag—you flurry one so.   80

FAG: Come, come, Lucy, here's no one by—so a little less
    simplicity, with a grain or two more sincerity, if you
    please.——You play false with us, madam.—I saw you
    give the baronet a letter.—My master shall know this—
    and if he don't call him out[1]—I will.   85

LUCY: Ha! ha! ha! you gentlemen's gentlemen are so hasty.
    — That letter was from Mrs. Malaprop, simpleton.—She
    is taken with Sir Lucius's address.[2]

FAG: How! what tastes some people have!—Why, I suppose
    I have walked by her window an hundred times.——But   90
    what says our young lady? Any message to my master?

LUCY: Sad news, Mr. Fag!—A worse rival than Acres!—
    Sir Anthony Absolute has proposed his son.

FAG: What, Captain Absolute?

LUCY: Even so.—I overheard it all.   95

FAG: Ha! ha! ha!—very good, faith.—Good-bye, Lucy, I
    must away with this news.

LUCY: Well—you may laugh—but it is true, I assure you.
    [*Going*] But—Mr. Fag—tell your master not to be cast
    down by this.   100

FAG: O he'll be so disconsolate!

LUCY: And charge him not to think of quarrelling with
    young Absolute.

FAG: Never fear!—never fear!

LUCY: Be sure—bid him keep up his spirits.   105

FAG: We will—we will.   *Exeunt severally*

[1] Challenge to a duel.   [2] Bearing.

Act III scene i

The North Parade

Enter ABSOLUTE

ABSOLUTE: 'Tis just as Fag told me, indeed.—Whimsical enough, faith! My father wants to *force* me to marry the very girl I am plotting to run away with!—He must not know of my connection with her yet awhile.—He has too summary a method of proceeding in these matters. How- 5 ever, I'll read my recantation instantly.—My conversion is something sudden, indeed—but I can assure him it is very *sincere*.——So, so—here he comes.—He looks plaguy gruff. [*Steps aside*]

Enter SIR ANTHONY

[SIR ANTHONY]: No—I'll die sooner than forgive him. 10 —*Die*, did I say? I'll live these fifty years to plague him.— At our last meeting, his impudence had almost put me out of temper.—An obstinate, passionate, self-willed boy! —Who can he take after? This is my return for getting him before all his brothers and sisters!—for putting him, 15 at twelve years old, into a marching regiment, and allow- ing him fifty pounds a-year, beside his pay ever since!— But I have done with him;—he's anybody's son for me.— I never will see him more,—never—never—never— never! 20

ABSOLUTE: Now for a penitential face.

SIR ANTHONY: Fellow, get out of my way.

ABSOLUTE: Sir, you see a penitent before you.

SIR ANTHONY: I see an impudent scoundrel before me.

ABSOLUTE: A sincere penitent.—I am come, sir, to acknowledge my error, and to submit entirely to your will.

SIR ANTHONY: What's that?

ABSOLUTE: I have been revolving, and reflecting, and considering on your past goodness, and kindness, and condescension[1] to me.

SIR ANTHONY: Well, sir?

ABSOLUTE: I have been likewise weighing and balancing what you were pleased to mention concerning duty, and obedience, and authority.

SIR ANTHONY: Well, puppy?

ABSOLUTE: Why then, sir, the result of my reflection is—a resolution to sacrifice every inclination of my own to your satisfaction.

SIR ANTHONY: Why now, you talk sense—absolute sense —I never heard anything more sensible in my life.— Confound you, you shall be *Jack* again!

ABSOLUTE: I am happy in the appellation.

SIR ANTHONY: Why, then, Jack, my dear Jack, I will now inform you—who the lady really is.—Nothing but your passion and violence, you silly fellow, prevented my telling you at first. Prepare, Jack, for wonder and rapture— —prepare.——What think you of Miss Lydia Languish?

ABSOLUTE: Languish! What, the Languishes of Worcestershire?

SIR ANTHONY: Worcestershire! No. Did you never meet Mrs. Malaprop and her niece, Miss Languish, who came into our country just before you were last ordered to your regiment?

ABSOLUTE: Malaprop! Languish! I don't remember ever to

[1] Affability.

have heard the names before. Yet stay,—I think I do   55
recollect something.——*Languish! Languish!* She squints,
don't she?—A little, red-haired girl?

SIR ANTHONY: Squints?—A red-haired girl!—Z——ds!
no.

ABSOLUTE: Then I must have forgot; it can't be the same   60
person.

SIR ANTHONY: Jack! Jack! what think you of blooming,
love-breathing seventeen?

ABSOLUTE: As to that, sir, I am quite indifferent.—If I can
please you in the matter, 'tis all I desire.   65

SIR ANTHONY: Nay, but Jack, such eyes! such eyes! so
innocently wild! so bashfully irresolute! Not a glance but
speaks and kindles some thought of love! Then, Jack, her
cheeks, Jack! so deeply blushing at the insinuations of her
tell-tale eyes! Then, Jack, her lips!—O Jack, lips smiling   70
at their own discretion; and if not smiling, more sweetly
pouting; more lovely in sullenness!

ABSOLUTE: [*aside*]: That's she, indeed.—Well done, old
gentleman!

SIR ANTHONY: Then, Jack, her neck![1]—O Jack! Jack!   75

ABSOLUTE: And which is to be mine, sir, the niece or the
aunt?

SIR ANTHONY: Why, you unfeeling, insensible puppy, I
despise you! When I was of your age, such a description
would have made me fly like a rocket![2] The *aunt*, indeed!   80
—Odds life! when I ran away with your mother, I would
not have touched anything old or ugly to gain an empire.

ABSOLUTE: Not to please your father, sir?

SIR ANTHONY: To please my father!——Z——ds! not to
please——O, my father!—Oddso!—yes—yes; if my   85

---

[1] Neck, shoulders, and upper part of breasts, as exposed in the fashion of the
day.
[2] A firework.

father, indeed, had desired—that's quite another matter.—
Though he wa'n't the indulgent father that I am, Jack.

ABSOLUTE: I dare say not, sir.

SIR ANTHONY: But, Jack, you are not sorry to find your
mistress is so beautiful.   90

ABSOLUTE: Sir, I repeat it; if I please you in this affair, 'tis all
I desire. Not that I think a woman the worse for being
handsome; but, sir, if you please to recollect, you before
hinted something about a hump or two, one eye, and a
few more graces of that kind.—Now, without being very   95
nice, I own I should rather choose a wife of mine to have
the usual number of limbs, and a limited quantity of back:
and tho *one* eye may be very agreeable, yet as the
prejudice has always run in favour of *two*, I would not
wish to affect a singularity in that article.   100

SIR ANTHONY: What a phlegmatic[1] sot it is! Why, sirrah,
you're an anchorite![2]—a vile, insensible stock.[3]—You a
soldier!—you're a walking block, fit only to dust the
company's regimentals on!—Odd's life! I've a great mind
to marry the girl myself!   105

ABSOLUTE: I am entirely at your disposal, sir; if you should
think of addressing Miss Languish yourself, I suppose you
would have me marry the aunt; or if you should change
your mind, and take the old lady—'tis the same to me—
I'll marry the niece.   110

SIR ANTHONY: Upon my word, Jack, thou'rt either a very
great hypocrite, or——but, come, I know your indifference on such a subject must be all a lie—I'm sure it must—
come, now—damn your demure face!—come, confess,
Jack—you have been lying—ha'n't you? You have been   115
playing the hypocrite, hey?—I'll never forgive you, if
you ha'n't been lying and playing the hypocrite.

[1] Sluggish.   [2] Hermit.
[3] Heavy block of wood.

ABSOLUTE: I'm sorry, sir, that the respect and duty which I
bear to you should be so mistaken.

SIR ANTHONY: Hang your respect and duty! But, come   120
along with me, I'll write a note to Mrs. Malaprop, and
you shall visit the lady directly. Her eyes shall be the
Promethean[1] torch to you—come along, I'll never forgive
you if you don't come back, stark mad with rapture and
impatience—if you don't, egad, I'll marry the girl myself!   125

Exeunt

Scene ii

JULIA's *dressing-room*

FAULKLAND *solus*

FAULKLAND: They told me Julia would return directly; I
wonder she is not yet come!—How mean does this captious,
unsatisfied temper of mine appear to my cooler judgment!
Yet I know not that I indulge it in any other point:—but
on this one subject, and to this one subject, whom I think   5
I love beyond my life, I am ever ungenerously fretful, and
madly capricious!—I am conscious of it—yet I cannot
correct myself! What tender, honest joy sparkled in her
eyes when we met!—How delicate was the warmth of her
expressions!—I was ashamed to appear less happy—   10
though I had come resolved to wear a face of coolness and
upbraiding. Sir Anthony's presence prevented my pro-
posed expostulations:—yet I must be satisfied that she has
not been so *very* happy in my absence.—She is coming!—
Yes!—I know the nimbleness of her tread when she   15
thinks her impatient Faulkland counts the moments of her
stay.

[1] Prometheus stole fire from heaven to animate his men of clay. Lydia's eyes
shall give Jack life.

Enter JULIA

JULIA: I had not hoped to see you again so soon.

FAULKLAND: Could I, Julia, be contented with my first welcome—restrained as we were by the presence of a third person?   20

JULIA: O Faulkland, when your kindness can make me thus happy, let me not think that I discovered something of coldness in your first salutation.

FAULKLAND: 'Twas but your fancy, Julia.—I *was* rejoiced   25
to see you—to see you in such health.—Sure I had no cause for coldness?

JULIA: Nay then, I see you have taken something ill.—You must not conceal from me what it is.

FAULKLAND: Well then—shall I own to you that my joy   30
at hearing of your health and arrival here, by your neigh-bour Acres, was somewhat damped, by his dwelling much on high spirits you had enjoyed in Devonshire—on your mirth—your singing—dancing, and I know not what!—For such is my temper, Julia, that I should regard every   35
mirthful moment in your absence as a treason to constancy:
—The mutual tear that steals down the cheek of parting lovers is a compact, that no smile shall live there till they meet again.

JULIA: Must I never cease to tax my Faulkland with this   40
teasing minute caprice?—Can the idle reports of a silly boor weigh in your breast against my tried affection?

FAULKLAND: They have no weight with me, Julia: no, no—I am happy if you have been so—yet only say, that you did not sing with *mirth*—say that you *thought* of Faulkland in   45
the dance.

JULIA: I never can be happy in your absence.—If I wear a countenance of content, it is to show that my mind holds no doubt of my Faulkland's truth.——If I seemed sad—it

were to make malice triumph, and say, that I had fixed my   50
heart on one, who left me to lament his roving, and my
own credulity.—Believe me, Faulkland, I mean not to
upbraid you, when I say, that I have often dressed sorrow
in smiles, lest my friends should guess whose unkindness
had caused my tears.   55

FAULKLAND: You were ever all goodness to me.—O, I am a
brute when I but admit a doubt of your true constancy!

JULIA: If ever, without such cause from you, as I will not
suppose possible, you find my affections veering but a
point,[1] may I become a proverbial scoff for levity, and base   60
ingratitude.

FAULKLAND: Ah! Julia, that last word is grating to me. I
would I had no title to[2] your *gratitude!* Search your heart,
Julia; perhaps what you have mistaken for love, is but
the warm effusion of a too thankful heart!   65

JULIA: For what quality must I love you?

FAULKLAND: For no quality! To regard me for any quality
of mind or understanding, were only to *esteem* me. And for
person—I have often wished myself deformed, to be convinced that I owed no obligation *there* for any part of your   70
affection.

JULIA: Where Nature has bestowed a show of nice attention
in the features of a man, he should laugh at it, as misplaced.
I have seen men, who in *this* vain article perhaps might rank
above you; but my heart has never asked my eyes if it were   75
so or not.

FAULKLAND: Now this is not well from *you*, Julia.—I
despise person in a man.—Yet if you loved me as I wish,
though I were an Æthiop,[3] you'd think none so fair.

[1] One of the thirty-two points of the compass, i.e. $11°\ 15'$.   [2] Claim upon.

[3] Like 'eremite', this word belongs to poetic language. The allusion here is to
absolute contrast, as in *Romeo and Juliet*, I. v. 49 ('Like a rich jewel in an Ethiop's
ear'), or *Love's Labour's Lost*, IV. iii. 116–17 ('Thou for whom Jove would swear/
Juno but an Ethiop were').

JULIA: I see you are determined to be unkind.—The *contract*   80
which my poor father bound us in gives you more than a
lover's privilege.

FAULKLAND: Again, Julia, you raise ideas that feed and
justify my doubts.—I would not have been more free—
no—I am proud of my restraint.——Yet—yet—perhaps   85
your high respect alone for this solemn compact has
fettered your inclinations, which else had made a worthier
choice.—How shall I be sure, had you remained unbound
in thought and promise, that I should still have been the
object of your persevering love?   90

JULIA: Then try me now.—Let us be free as strangers as to
what is past:—*my* heart will not feel more liberty!

FAULKLAND: There now! so hasty, Julia! so anxious to be
free!—If your love for me were fixed and ardent, you
would not lose your hold, even tho' I wished it!   95

JULIA: O, you torture me to the heart!—I cannot
bear it.

FAULKLAND: I do not mean to distress you.—If I loved you
less, I should never give you an uneasy moment.—But hear
me.—All my fretful doubts arise from this—Women are   100
not used to weigh, and separate the motives of their
affections:—the cold dictates of prudence, gratitude, or
filial duty, may sometimes be mistaken for the pleadings
of the heart.——I would not boast—yet let me say, that I
have neither age, person, or character, to found dislike on;   105
—my fortune such as few ladies could be charged with
indiscretion in the match.—O Julia! when *Love* receives
such countenance from *Prudence*, nice minds will be suspicious of its *birth*.

JULIA: I know not whither your insinuations would tend:—   110
but as they seem pressing to insult me—I will spare you
the regret of having done so.—I have given you no cause
for this!   *Exit in tears*

FAULKLAND: In tears! Stay, Julia: stay but for a moment.
——The door is fastened!—Julia;—my soul—but for one 115
moment:—I hear her sobbing!—'Sdeath! what a brute
am I to use her thus! Yet stay!—Aye—she is coming now:
—how little resolution there is in woman!—How a few
soft words can turn them!——No, faith!—she is *not* coming
either.——Why, Julia—my love—say but that you for- 120
give me—come but to tell me that.—Now, this is being
too resentful:—stay! she *is* coming too—I thought she
would—no *steadiness* in anything! her going away must
have been a mere trick then.—She sha'n't see that I was
hurt by it.—I'll affect indifference.—[*Hums a tune: then* 125
listens]——No—Z—ds! she's *not* coming!—nor don't
intend it, I suppose.—This is not *steadiness*, but *obstinacy!*
Yet I deserve it.—What, after so long an absence, to
quarrel with her tenderness!—'twas barbarous and unmanly!—I should be ashamed to see her now.—I'll wait till 130
her just resentment is abated—and when I distress her so
again, may I lose her for ever! and be linked instead to
some antique virago, whose gnawing passions, and long-
hoarded spleen, shall make me curse my folly half the day,
and all the night!   *Exit* 135

Scene iii

MRS. MALAPROP's *lodgings*

MRS. MALAPROP, *with a letter in her hand, and*
CAPTAIN ABSOLUTE

MRS. MALAPROP: Your being Sir Anthony's son, Captain,
would itself be a sufficient accommodation;[1]—but from

---

[1] Recommendation.

the ingenuity[1] of your appearance, I am convinced you deserve the character here given of you.

ABSOLUTE: Permit me to say, madam, that as I never yet 5
have had the pleasure of seeing Miss Languish, my principal inducement in this affair at present, is the honour of
being allied to Mrs. Malaprop; of whose intellectual
accomplishments, elegant manners, and unaffected learning, no tongue is silent. 10

MRS. MALAPROP: Sir, you do me infinite honour!—I beg,
Captain, you'll be seated.—[Sit]—Ah! few gentlemen
now-a-days know how to value the ineffectual[2] qualities
in a woman!—few think how a little knowledge becomes
a gentlewoman! Men have no sense now but for the 15
worthless flower of beauty!

ABSOLUTE: It is but too true, indeed, ma'am.—Yet I fear
our ladies should share the blame—they think our
admiration of *beauty* so great, that knowledge in *them*
would be superfluous. Thus, like garden-trees, they seldom 20
show fruit, till time has fobbed them of the more specious
blossom.—Few, like Mrs. Malaprop and the orange-tree,
are rich in both at once!

MRS. MALAPROP: Sir—you overpower me with good
breeding.—He is the very pine-apple[3] of politeness!— 25
You are not ignorant, Captain, that this giddy girl has
somehow contrived to fix her affections on a beggarly,
strolling,[4] eaves-dropping Ensign, whom none of us have
seen, and nobody knows anything of.

ABSOLUTE: O, I have heard the silly affair before.—I'm not 30
at all prejudiced against her on *that* account.

MRS. MALAPROP: You are very good, and very considerate,
Captain.—I am sure I have done everything in my power
since I exploded[5] the affair! Long ago I laid my positive

---

[1] Ingenuousness.   [2] Intellectual.   [3] Pinnacle.
[4] Tramping.   [5] Exposed.

conjunctions[1] on her never to think on the fellow again; 35
—I have since laid Sir Anthony's preposition[2] before her;
—but, I am sorry to say, she seems resolved to decline
every particle[3] that I enjoin[4] her.

ABSOLUTE: It must be very distressing, indeed, ma'am.

MRS. MALAPROP: Oh! it gives me the hydrostatics[5] to such 40
a degree!—I thought she had persisted[6] from corresponding with him; but behold this very day, I have inter-
ceded[7] another letter from the fellow! I believe I have it
in my pocket.

ABSOLUTE [aside]: O the devil! my last note. 45

MRS. MALAPROP: Aye, here it is.

ABSOLUTE [aside]: Aye, my note, indeed! O the little trait-
ress Lucy.

MRS. MALAPROP: There, perhaps you may know the
writing.   [Gives him the letter] 50

ABSOLUTE: I think I have seen the hand before—yes, I
certainly must have seen this hand before:——

MRS. MALAPROP: Nay, but read it Captain.

ABSOLUTE [reads]: 'My soul's idol, my adored Lydia!'—Very
tender, indeed!

MRS. MALAPROP: Tender! aye, and profane, too, o' my 55
conscience!

ABSOLUTE: 'I am excessively alarmed at the intelligence you
send me, the more so as my new rival'——

MRS. MALAPROP: That's you, sir. 60

ABSOLUTE: 'has universally the character of being an accomplished gentleman, and a man of honour.'——Well, that's
handsome enough.

MRS. MALAPROP: O, the fellow had some design in
writing so. 65

---

[1] Injunctions.   [2] Proposition.   [3] Article.
[4] Inflict upon.   [5] Hysterics.   [6] Desisted.
[7] Intercepted.

ABSOLUTE: That he had, I'll answer for him, ma'am.

MRS. MALAPROP: But go on, sir—you'll see presently.

ABSOLUTE: '*As for the old weather-beaten she-dragon who guards you*'—Who can he mean by that?

MRS. MALAPROP: *Me*, Sir—*me*—he means *me*, there— what do you think now?—But go on a little further.

ABSOLUTE: Impudent scoundrel!—'*it shall go hard but I will elude her vigilance, as I am told that the same ridiculous vanity which makes her dress up her coarse features, and deck her dull chat with hard words which she don't understand*'——

MRS. MALAPROP: There, sir! an attack upon my language! What do you think of that?—an aspersion upon my parts of speech! Was ever such a brute! Sure if I reprehend[1] anything in this world, it is the use of my oracular[2] tongue, and a nice derangement[3] of epitaphs![4]

ABSOLUTE: He deserves to be hanged and quartered![5] Let me see—'*same ridiculous vanity*'—

MRS. MALAPROP: You need not read it again, sir.

ABSOLUTE: I beg pardon, ma'am——'*does also lay her open to the grossest deceptions from flattery and pretended admiration*' —an impudent coxcomb![6]——'*so that I have a scheme to see you shortly with the old harridan's consent, and even to make her a go-between in our interviews.*'—Was ever such assurance!

MRS. MALAPROP: Did you ever hear anything like it?— he'll elude my vigilance, will he?—yes, yes! ha! ha! he's very likely to enter these doors!—we'll try who can plot best!

ABSOLUTE: So we will, ma'am—so we will. Ha! ha! ha! a conceited puppy, ha! ha! ha!——Well, but Mrs. Malaprop, as the girl seems so infatuated by this fellow, suppose

---

[1] Comprehend.   [2] Vernacular.
[3] Arrangement.   [4] Epithets
[5] Cut up into four pieces, a fate reserved for traitors.
[6] Conceited ass.

you were to wink at her corresponding with him for a
little time—let her even plot an elopement with him—
then do you connive at her escape—while *I*, just in the
nick,[1] will have the fellow laid by the heels,[2] and fairly
contrive to carry her off in his stead.   100

MRS. MALAPROP: I am delighted with the scheme, never
   was anything better perpetrated!

ABSOLUTE: But, pray, could not I see the lady for a few
   minutes now?—I should like to try her temper a little.

MRS. MALAPROP: Why, I don't know—I doubt she is not   105
   prepared for a visit of this kind.—There is a decorum in
   these matters.

ABSOLUTE: O Lord! she won't mind *me*—only tell her
   Beverley——

MRS. MALAPROP: Sir!——   110

ABSOLUTE [*aside*]: Gently, good tongue.

MRS. MALAPROP: What did you say of Beverley?

ABSOLUTE: O, I was going to propose that you should tell
   her, by way of jest, that it was Beverley who was below—
   she'd come down fast enough then—ha! ha! ha!   115

MRS. MALAPROP: 'Twould be a trick she well deserves.—
   Besides you know the fellow tells her he'll get my consent
   to see her—ha! ha!—Let him if he can, I say again.—
   Lydia, come down here! [*Calling*]—He'll make me a *go-
   between in their interviews* !—ha! ha! ha!—Come down, I   120
   say, Lydia!—I don't wonder at your laughing, ha! ha! ha!
   —his impudence is truly ridiculous.

ABSOLUTE: 'Tis very ridiculous, upon my soul, ma'am,
   ha! ha! ha!

MRS. MALAPROP: The little hussy won't hear.—Well, I'll   125
   go and tell her at once who it is.—She shall know that
   Capt. Absolute is come to wait on her.—And I'll make
   her behave as becomes a young woman.

[1] Of time.   [2] Confine or put out of action.

ABSOLUTE: As you please, ma'am.

MRS. MALAPROP: For the present, Captain, your servant. 130
Ah! you've not done laughing yet, I see—*elude my
vigilance!*—yes, yes, ha! ha! ha!   *Exit*

ABSOLUTE: Ha! ha! ha! one would think now that I might
throw off all disguise at once, and seize my prize with
security—but such is Lydia's caprice, that to undeceive 135
were probably to lose her.—I'll see whether she knows
me.

[*Walks aside, and seems engaged in looking at the pictures*]

Enter LYDIA

LYDIA: What a scene am I now to go thro'! Surely nothing
can be more dreadful than to be obliged to listen to the
loathsome addresses of a stranger to one's heart.—I have 140
heard of girls persecuted as I am, who have appealed in
behalf of their favoured lover to the generosity of his
rival: suppose I were to try it—there stands the hated
rival—an officer too!—but O, how unlike my Beverley!
—I wonder he don't begin—truly he seems a very negli- 145
gent wooer!—quite at his ease, upon my word!—I'll speak
first.—[*Aloud.*] Mr. Absolute.

ABSOLUTE: Madam.

LYDIA: O heav'ns! Beverley!

ABSOLUTE: Hush!—hush, my life!—softly! Be not sur- 150
prised!

LYDIA: I am so astonished! and so terrified! and so
overjoyed!—For heav'n's sake! how came you
here?

ABSOLUTE: Briefly—I have deceived your aunt.—I was in- 155
formed that my new rival was to visit here this evening,
and contriving to have him kept away, have passed myself
on *her* for Capt. Absolute.

LYDIA: O, charming!—And she really takes you for young Absolute? 160

ABSOLUTE: O, she's convinced of it.

LYDIA: Ha! ha! ha! I can't forbear laughing to think how her sagacity is over-reached!

ABSOLUTE: But we trifle with our precious moments—such another opportunity may not occur—then let me now 165 conjure my kind, my condescending angel, to fix the time when I may rescue her from undeserved persecution, and with a licensed[1] warmth plead for my reward.

LYDIA: Will you then, Beverley, consent to forfeit that portion of my paltry wealth!—that burden on the wings of 170 love?

ABSOLUTE: O, come to me—rich only thus—in loveliness. —Bring no portion to me but thy love—'twill be generous in you, Lydia—for well you know, it is the only dower your poor Beverley can repay. 175

LYDIA: How persuasive are his words!—how charming will poverty be with him!

ABSOLUTE: Ah! my soul, what a life will we then live! Love shall be our idol and support! We will worship him with a monastic strictness; abjuring all worldly toys, to 180 centre every thought and action there.—Proud of calamity, we will enjoy the wreck of wealth; while the surrounding gloom of adversity shall make the flame of our pure love show doubly bright.—By heav'ns! I would fling all goods of fortune from me with a prodigal hand, to enjoy the 185 scene where I might clasp my Lydia to my bosom, and say, the world affords no smile to me—but here. [*Embracing her*]——[*Aside*] If she holds out now the devil is in it!

LYDIA: Now could I fly with him to the Antipodes! but my 190 persecution is not yet come to a crisis.

---

[1] Married.

Enter MRS. MALAPROP, *listening*

MRS. MALAPROP [*aside*]: I am impatient to know how the little hussy deports herself.

ABSOLUTE: So pensive, Lydia!—is then your warmth abated?

MRS. MALAPROP[*aside*]: Warmth abated!—So! she has been 195
in a passion, I suppose.

LYDIA: No—nor ever can while I have life.

MRS. MALAPROP: [*aside*]: An ill-tempered little devil!—
She'll be in a passion all her life—will she?

LYDIA: Think not the idle threats of my ridiculous aunt 200
can ever have any weight with me.

MRS. MALAPROP [*aside*]: Very dutiful, upon my word!

LYDIA: Let her choice be *Captain Absolute*, but Beverley is mine.

MRS. MALAPROP[*aside*]: I am astonished at her assurance!— 205
to his face—this is his face!

ABSOLUTE: Thus then let me enforce my suit.   [*Kneeling*]

MRS. MALAPROP [*aside*]: Aye—poor young man!—down
on his knees entreating for pity!—I can contain no longer.
—[*Aloud*] Why, thou vixen!—I have overheard you.   210

ABSOLUTE [*aside*]: O, confound her vigilance!

MRS. MALAPROP: Capt. *Absolute*—I know not how to
apologize for her shocking rudeness.

ABSOLUTE [*aside*]: So—all's safe, I find.—[*Aloud*] I have
hopes, madam, that time will bring the young lady—— 215

MRS. MALAPROP: O, there's nothing to be hoped for from
her! She's as headstrong as an allegory[1] on the banks of
Nile.

LYDIA: Nay, madam, what do you charge me with now?

MRS. MALAPROP: Why, thou unblushing rebel—didn't 220
you tell this gentleman to his face that you loved another
better?—didn't you say you never would be his?

[1] Alligator.

LYDIA: No, madam—I did not.

MRS. MALAPROP: Good heav'ns! what assurance!— Lydia, Lydia, you ought to know that lying don't become 225 a young woman!—Didn't you boast that *Beverley*—that stroller[1] *Beverley*—possessed your heart?—Tell me that, I say.

LYDIA: 'Tis true, ma'am, and none but *Beverley*——

MRS. MALAPROP: Hold;—hold, Assurance!—you shall not be so rude. 230

ABSOLUTE: Nay, pray Mrs. Malaprop, don't stop the young lady's speech:—she's very welcome to talk thus—it does not hurt *me* in the least, I assure you.

MRS. MALAPROP: You are *too* good, Captain—*too* amiably patient—but come with me, miss.—Let us see you again 235 soon, Captain.—Remember what we have fixed.

ABSOLUTE: I shall, ma'am.

MRS. MALAPROP: Come, take a graceful leave of the gentleman.

LYDIA: May every blessing wait on my *Beverley*, my loved 240 *Bev*——

MRS. MALAPROP: Hussy! I'll choke the word in your throat!—come along—come along.

Exeunt severally, BEVERLEY (ABSOLUTE) *kissing his hand to* LYDIA—MRS. MALAPROP *stopping her from speaking*

Scene iv

ACRES'S *lodgings*

ACRES *and* DAVID

ACRES *as just dressed*

ACRES: Indeed, David—do you think I become it so?

DAVID: You are quite another creature, believe me, master,

---

[1] Tramp or itinerant actor.

by the Mass! an' we've any luck we shall see the Devon
monkeyrony[1] in all the print-shops[2] in Bath!

ACRES: Dress *does* make a difference, David.   5

DAVID: 'Tis all in all, I think.—Difference! why, an' you
were to go now to Clod-Hall,[3] I am certain the old lady
wouldn't know you: Master Butler wouldn't believe his
own eyes, and Mrs. Pickle would cry, 'Lard presarve[4]
me!'—our dairy-maid would come giggling to the door,   10
and I warrant Dolly Tester,[5] your Honour's favourite,
would blush like my waistcoat.—Oons![6] I'll hold a gallon,[7]
there a'n't a dog in the house but would bark, and question
whether *Phyllis* would wag a hair of her tail!

ACRES: Aye, David, there's nothing like polishing.   15

DAVID: So I says of your Honour's boots; but the boy never
heeds me!

ACRES: But, David, has Mr. De-la-Grace[8] been here? I must
rub up my balancing, and chasing, and boring.[9]

DAVID: I'll call again, sir.   20

ACRES: Do—and see if there are any letters for me at the
post-office.

DAVID: I will.—By the Mass, I can't help looking at your
head!—If I hadn't been by at the cooking, I wish I
may die if I should have known the dish again   25
myself!   *Exit*

---

[1] Both 'monkey' and 'macaroni' were used at this period for 'fop'. Cf. 'A slim
beast made for shew/Which the men call a monkey, but ladies a beau!' (Anthony
Pasquin, *A Postscript to the New Bath Guide* (1790), p. 62).

[2] Shops selling engraved portraits, views, and caricatures.

[3] Acres's house in rural Devonshire.

[4] Dialect for 'Lord preserve'.

[5] From 'tester-bed', a bed with a canopy. Dolly was clearly a chambermaid.

[6] From 'Zounds!': see p. 31, n. 2.

[7] I'll wager a gallon of ale that the dogs will not know you.

[8] See p. 32, n. 1.

[9] Dance movements: 'boring' is from the French 'bourrée', and 'chasing' from
'chassée'. 'Balancing' is to move in opposite directions from one's partner.

ACRES *comes forward, practising a dancing step*

ACRES: Sink, slide—coupee![1]—Confound the first inventors
of cotillons![2] say I—they are as bad as algebra to us
country gentlemen.—I can walk a minuet[3] easy enough
when I'm forced!—and I have been accounted a good
stick in a country-dance.—Odds jigs and tabors![4]—I never   30
valued[5] your cross-over to couple—figure in—right and
left—and I'd foot it with e'er a captain in the county!—
but these outlandish heathen allemandes[6] and cotillons
are quite beyond me!—I shall never prosper at 'em, that's
sure.—Mine are true-born English legs—they don't   35
understand their curst French lingo!—their *pas* this, and *pas*
that, and *pas* t'other!—Damn me! my feet don't like to
be called paws! no, 'tis certain I have most antigallican[7]
toes!

Enter SERVANT

SERVANT: Here is Sir Lucius O'Trigger to wait on you, sir.   40
ACRES: Show him in.

Enter SIR LUCIUS

SIR LUCIUS: Mr. Acres, I am delighted to embrace you.
ACRES: My dear Sir Lucius, I kiss your hands.
SIR LUCIUS: Pray, my friend, what has brought you so sud-
denly to Bath?   45
ACRES: Faith! I have followed Cupid's Jack-a-Lantern,[8] and
find myself in a quagmire at last.—In short, I have been
very ill-used, Sir Lucius.—I don't choose to mention
names, but look on me as on a very ill-used gentleman.

---

[1] Cross over.   [2] See 'cotillion', p. 55, n. 1.   [3] See p. 55, n. 1.
[4] Small drums.   [5] Gave much thought to.   [6] A lively German dance.
[7] Hostile to everything French.
[8] Ignis fatuus, a flame of marsh-gas, which misleads travellers.

SIR LUCIUS: Pray, what is the case?—I ask no names.   50
ACRES: Mark me, Sir Lucius, I fall as deep as need be in love
with a young lady—her friends take my part—I follow
her to Bath—send word of my arrival, and receive
answer, that the lady is to be otherwise disposed of.—
This, Sir Lucius, I call being ill-used.   55
SIR LUCIUS: Very ill, upon my conscience.—Pray, can you
divine the cause of it?
ACRES. Why, there's the matter: she has another lover, one
Beverley, who, I am told, is now in Bath.—Odds slanders
and lies! he must be at the bottom of it.   60
SIR LUCIUS: A rival in the case, is there?—And you think
he has supplanted you unfairly?
ACRES: Unfairly!—to be sure he has.—He never could have
done it fairly.
SIR LUCIUS: Then sure you know what is to be done!   65
ACRES: Not I, upon my soul!
SIR LUCIUS: We wear no swords here,[1] but you understand
me.
ACRES: What! fight him?
SIR LUCIUS: Aye, to be sure: what can I mean else?   70
ACRES: But he has given me no provocation.
SIR LUCIUS: Now, I think he has given you the greatest
provocation in the world.—Can a man commit a more
heinous offence against another than to fall in love with
the same woman? O, by my soul, it is the most unpardon-   75
able breach of friendship!
ACRES: Breach of friendship! Aye, aye: but I have no
acquaintance with this man. I never saw him in my life.
SIR LUCIUS: That's no argument at all—he has the less
right then to take such a liberty.   80
ACRES: 'Gad, that's true.—I grow full of anger, Sir Lucius!

[1] Beau Nash, Master of Ceremonies at Bath, forbade the wearing of swords 'as
they often tore the ladies' clothes'.

—I fire apace! Odds hilts and blades![1] I find a man may
have a deal of valour in him and not know it! But
couldn't I contrive to have a little right of my side?

SIR LUCIUS: What the devil signifies *right* when your *honour*   85
is concerned? Do you think *Achilles*,[2] or my little
Alexander the Great[3] ever inquired where the right lay?
No, by my soul, they drew their broadswords, and left
the lazy sons of peace to settle the justice of it.

ACRES: Your words are a grenadier's[4] march to my heart! I   90
believe courage must be catching!—I certainly do feel a
kind of valour rising as it were—a kind of courage, as I
may say.——Odds flints, pans,[5] and triggers! I'll challenge him directly.

SIR LUCIUS: Ah, my little friend! if we had *Blunderbuss-Hall*   95
here—I could show you a range of ancestry, in the
O'Trigger line, that would furnish the new room;[6] every
one of whom had killed this man!—For though the
mansion-house and dirty acres have slipt through my
fingers, I thank heav'n our honour, and the family-   100
pictures, are as fresh as ever.

ACRES: O Sir Lucius! I have had ancestors too! every man
of 'em colonel or captain in the militia!—Odds balls and
barrels! say no more—I'm braced for it—The thunder of
your words has soured the milk of human kindness[7] in   105
my breast!——Z—ds! as the man in the play says, 'I
could do such deeds'—[8]

---

[1] Cf. Sir Joseph Wittol's oath in Congreve's *The Old Bachelor* (1693), II. i:
'Gads-Daggers-Belts-Blades-and Scabbards.'

[2] Champion of the Greeks in the Trojan War.

[3] 356–323 B.C., King of Macedon: 'little' is an endearment.

[4] Acres seems to have connected Achilles and Alexander with the first line of
'The British Grenadiers': 'Some talk of Alexander, and some of Hercules.'

[5] Part of a gun's firelock holding the powder.

[6] The Upper Assembly rooms, east of the Circus and opened in 1771.

[7] From *Macbeth*, I. v.

[8] Possibly misquoting Lear's 'I will do such things' (II. iv).

SIR LUCIUS: Come, come, there must be no passion at all in the case—these things should always be done civilly.

ACRES: I must be in a passion, Sir Lucius—I must be in a 110 rage.—Dear Sir Lucius, let me be in a rage, if you love me. —Come, here's pen and paper. [*Sits down to write*] I would the ink were red!—Indite, I say indite!—How shall I begin? Odds bullets and blades! I'll write a good bold hand, however. 115

SIR LUCIUS: Pray compose yourself.

ACRES: Come—now shall I begin with an oath? Do, Sir Lucius, let me begin with a damme.

SIR LUCIUS: Pho! pho! do the thing decently and like a Christian. Begin now,—'Sir'—— 120

ACRES: That's too civil by half.

SIR LUCIUS: '*To prevent the confusion that might arise*'—

ACRES: Well——

SIR LUCIUS: '*From our both addressing the same lady*'

ACRES: Aye—there's the reason—'*same lady*'—Well—— 125

SIR LUCIUS: '*I shall expect the honor of your company*'——

ACRES: Z——ds! I'm not asking him to dinner.

SIR LUCIUS: Pray be easy.

ACRES: Well then—'*honour of your company*'——

SIR LUCIUS: '*To settle our pretensions*'— 130

ACRES: Well—

SIR LUCIUS: Let me see—aye, *King's-Mead-Fields* will do— '*in King's-Mead-Fields.*'

ACRES: So that's done.—Well, I'll fold it up presently; my own crest—a hand and dagger shall be the seal. 135

SIR LUCIUS: You see now this little explanation will put a stop at once to all confusion or misunderstanding that might arise between you.

ACRES: Aye, we fight to prevent any misunderstanding.

SIR LUCIUS: Now, I'll leave you to fix your own time.— 140 Take my advice, and you'll decide it this evening if you

can; then let the worst come of it, 'twill be off your mind
to-morrow.

ACRES: Very true.

SIR LUCIUS: So I shall see nothing more of you, unless it be   145
by letter, till the evening.—I would do myself the honour
to carry your message; but, to tell you a secret, I believe
I shall have just such another affair on my own hands.
There is a gay captain here, who put a jest on me lately
at the expense of my country, and I only want to fall in   150
with the gentleman, to call him out.

ACRES: By my valour, I should like to see you fight first!
Odds life! I should like to see you kill him, if it was only
to get a little lesson.

SIR LUCIUS: I shall be very proud of instructing you.—Well   155
for the present—but remember now, when you meet your
antagonist, do everything in a mild and agreeable manner.
—Let your courage be as keen, but at the same time as
polished as your sword.   *Exeunt severally*

Act IV scene i

DAVID: Then, by the Mass, sir! I would do no such thing—
ne'er a Sir Lucius O'Trigger in the kingdom should make
me fight, when I wa'n't so minded. Oons! what will the
old lady say, when she hears o't!

ACRES: Ah! David, if you had heard Sir Lucius!—Odds   5
sparks and flames! he would have roused your valour.

DAVID: Not he, indeed. I hates such bloodthirsty cormor-
ants.[1] Look'ee, master, if you'd wanted a bout at boxing,
quarter-staff, or short-staff,[2] I should never be the man to
bid you cry off: but for your curst sharps and snaps,[3] I   10
never knew any good come of 'em.

ACRES: But my honour, David, my honour! I must be very
careful of my honour.

DAVID: Aye, by the Mass! and I would be very careful of
it; and I think in return my *honour* couldn't do less than to   15
be very careful of *me*.

ACRES: Odds blades! David, no gentleman will ever risk
the loss of his honour!

DAVID: I say then, it would be but civil in *honour* never to
risk the loss of a *gentleman*.—Look'ee, master, this *honour*   20

---

[1] A large, greedy bird.
[2] The short-staff was a cudgel, and the quarter-staff a long pole tipped with
iron.
[3] Sharp swords and snapping pistols.

seems to me to be a marvellous false friend; aye, truly, a
very courtier-like servant.—Put the case, I was a gentleman (which, thank God, no one can say of me); well—my
honour makes me quarrel with another gentleman of my
acquaintance.—So—we fight. (Pleasant enough that) 25
Boh!—I kill him—(the more's my luck). Now, pray who
gets the profit[1] of it?—Why, my *honour*.—But put the
case that he kills me!—by the Mass! I go to the worms,
and my honour whips over to my enemy!

ACRES: No, David—in that case!—Odds crowns and 30
laurels! your honour follows you to the grave.

DAVID: Now, that's just the place where I could make a
shift to do without it.

ACRES: Z——ds, David, you're a coward!—It doesn't become my valour to listen to you.—What, shall I disgrace 35
my ancestors?—Think of that, David—think what it
would be to disgrace my ancestors!

DAVID: Under favour, the surest way of not disgracing
them, is to keep as long as you can out of their company.
Look'ee now, master, to go to them in such haste—with 40
an ounce of lead in your brains—I should think might as
well be let alone. Our ancestors are very good kind of
folks; but they are the last people I should choose to have
a visiting acquaintance with.

ACRES: But David, now, you don't think there is such very, 45
very, *very* great danger, hey?—Odds life! people often
fight without any mischief done!

DAVID: By the Mass, I think 'tis ten to one against you!—
Oons! here to meet some lion-headed fellow, I warrant,
with his d—n'd double-barrelled swords, and cut-and- 50
thrust pistols! Lord bless us! it makes me tremble to think
o't.—Those be such desperate bloody-minded weapons!
Well, I never could abide 'em!—from a child I never

---

[1] Cf. Falstaff on 'honour' in *King Henry IV, Pt. I*, V. i.

could fancy 'em!—I suppose there a'n't so merciless a beast
in the world as your loaded pistol! 55

ACRES: Z—ds! I *won't* be afraid!—Odds fire and fury! you
shan't make me afraid!—Here is the challenge, and I have
sent for my dear friend Jack Absolute to carry it
for me.

DAVID: Aye, i' the name of mischief, let *him* be the messen- 60
ger.—For my part, I wouldn't lend a hand to it for the best
horse in your stable. By the Mass! it don't look like another
letter! It is, as I may say, a designing and malicious-look-
ing letter!—and I warrant smells of gunpowder, like a
soldier's pouch!—Oons! I wouldn't swear it mayn't 65
go off!

ACRES: Out, you poltroon!—You ha'n't the valour of a
grasshopper.

DAVID: Well, I say no more—'twill be sad news, to be sure,
at Clod-Hall!—but I ha' done.—How Phyllis will howl 70
when she hears of it!—Aye, poor bitch, she little thinks
what shooting her master's going after!—And I warrant
old Crop, who has carried your honour, field and road,
these ten years, will curse the hour he was born.

[*Whimpering*]

ACRES: It won't do, David—I am determined to fight—so 75
get along, you coward, while I'm in the mind.

Enter SERVANT

SERVANT: Captain Absolute, sir.

ACRES: O! show him up. *Exit* SERVANT

DAVID: Well, heaven send we be all alive this time to-
morrow. 80

ACRES: What's that!—Don't provoke me, David!

DAVID: Good bye, master. [*Whimpering*]

ACRES: Get along, you cowardly, dastardly, croaking raven.

Exit DAVID

Enter ABSOLUTE

ABSOLUTE: What's the matter, Bob?

ACRES: A vile, sheep-hearted blockhead!—If I hadn't the   85
valour of St. George and the dragon to boot——

ABSOLUTE: But what did you want with me, Bob?

ACRES: O!—There——   [*Gives him the challenge*]

ABSOLUTE: '*To Ensign Beverley.*' [*Aside*] So—what's going
on now? [*Aloud*] Well, what's this?   90

ACRES: A challenge!

ABSOLUTE: Indeed!—Why, you won't fight him, will you,
Bob?

ACRES: 'Egad, but I will, Jack.—Sir Lucius has wrought me
to it. He has left me full of rage—and I'll fight this
evening, that so much good passion mayn't be   95
wasted.

ABSOLUTE: But what have I to do with this?

ACRES: Why, as I think you know something of this fellow,
I want you to find him out for me, and give him this
mortal defiance.

ABSOLUTE: Well, give it to me, and trust me he   100
gets it.

ACRES: Thank you, my dear friend, my dear Jack; but it is
giving you a great deal of trouble.

ABSOLUTE: Not in the least—I beg you won't mention it.
—No trouble in the world, I assure you.   105

ACRES: You are very kind.—What it is to have a friend!—
You couldn't be my second—could you, Jack?

ABSOLUTE: Why no, Bob—not in *this* affair—it would not
be quite so proper.[1]

ACRES: Well then, I must get my friend Sir Lucius. I shall   110
have your good wishes, however, Jack.

ABSOLUTE: Whenever he meets you, believe me.

---

[1] Because Absolute is believed to be a friend of Beverley, Acres's opponent.

Enter SERVANT

SERVANT: Sir Anthony Absolute is below, inquiring for the Captain.

ABSOLUTE: I'll come instantly.—Well, my little hero, suc- 115
cess attend you.   [*Going*]

ACRES: Stay—stay, Jack.—If Beverley should ask you what kind of a man your friend Acres is, do tell him I am a devil of a fellow—will you, Jack?

ABSOLUTE: To be sure I shall.—I'll say you are a determined 120
dog—hey, Bob?

ACRES: Aye, do, do—and if that frightens him, 'egad, per-haps he mayn't come. So tell him I generally kill a man a week; will you, Jack?

ABSOLUTE: I will, I will; I'll say you are called in the 125
country '*Fighting Bob!*'

ACRES: Right, right—'tis all to prevent mischief; for I don't want to take his life if I clear my honour.

ABSOLUTE: No!—that's very kind of you.

ACRES: Why, you don't wish me to kill him—do you, Jack? 130

ABSOLUTE: No, upon my soul, I do not.—But a devil of a fellow, hey?   [*Going*]

ACRES: True, true—but stay—stay, Jack—you may add that you never saw me in such a rage before—a most devouring rage!   135

ABSOLUTE: I will, I will.

ACRES: Remember, Jack—a determined dog!

ABSOLUTE: Aye, aye, '*Fighting Bob!*'   *Exeunt severally*

Scene ii

MRS. MALAPROP's *lodgings*

MRS. MALAPROP *and* LYDIA

MRS. MALAPROP: Why, thou perverse one!—tell me what

you can object to him?—Isn't he a handsome man?—tell
me that.—A genteel[1] man? a pretty figure of a man?

LYDIA [*aside*]: She little thinks whom she is praising!—
[*Aloud*] So is Beverley, ma'am.   5

MRS. MALAPROP: No caparisons,[2] miss, if you please!—
Caparisons don't become a young woman.—No!
Captain Absolute is indeed a fine gentleman!

LYDIA [*aside*]: Aye, the Captain Absolute *you* have seen.

MRS. MALAPROP: Then he's *so* well bred;—*so* full of alacrity,   10
and adulation!—and has *so much* to say for himself:—in
such good language, too!—His physiognomy[3] so gram-
matical!—Then his presence is so noble!—I protest, when
I saw him, I thought of what Hamlet says in the play:—
'Hesperian curls!—the front of *Job* himself!—an eye, like   15
March, to threaten at command!—a station, like Harry
Mercury, new'[4]—something about kissing—on a hill—
however, the similitude[5] struck me directly.

LYDIA [*aside*]: How enraged she'll be presently when she
discovers her mistake!   20

Enter SERVANT

SERVANT: Sir Anthony and Captain Absolute are below,
ma'am.

MRS. MALAPROP: Show them up here.   *Exit* SERVANT
Now, Lydia, I insist on your behaving as becomes a young
woman.—Show your good breeding at least, though you   25
have forgot your duty.

---

[1] Refined.   [2] Comparisons.   [3] Phraseology.
[4] From *Hamlet*, III, iv:

> Hyperion's curls; the front of Jove himself;
> An eye like Mars, to threaten and command;
> A station like the herald Mercury
> New-lighted on a heaven-kissing hill.

[5] Simile.

LYDIA: Madam, I have told you my resolution!—I shall not only give him no encouragement, but I won't even speak to, or look at him.

[*Flings herself into a chair, with her face from the door*]

Enter SIR ANTHONY *and* ABSOLUTE

SIR ANTHONY: Here we are, Mrs. Malaprop, come to   30
mitigate the frowns of unrelenting beauty—and difficulty enough I had to bring this fellow.—I don't know what's the matter; but if I hadn't held him by force, he'd have given me the slip.

MRS. MALAPROP: You have infinite trouble, Sir Anthony,   35
in the affair. I am ashamed for the cause!—[*Aside to her*]
Lydia, Lydia, rise, I beseech you!—pay your respects!

SIR ANTHONY: I hope, madam, that Miss Languish has reflected on the worth of this gentleman, and the regard due to her aunt's choice, and *my* alliance.—[*Aside to him*]   40
Now, Jack, speak to her!

ABSOLUTE [*aside*]: What the d—l shall I do!—[*Aloud*] You see, sir, she won't even look at me, whilst you are here.—
I knew she wouldn't!—I told you so.—Let me entreat you, sir, to leave us together!   45

[ABSOLUTE *seems to expostulate with his father*]

LYDIA [*aside*]: I wonder I ha'n't heard my aunt exclaim yet! Sure she can't have looked at him!—perhaps their regimentals are alike, and she is something blind.

SIR ANTHONY: I say, sir, I won't stir a foot yet!

MRS. MALAPROP: I am sorry to say, Sir Anthony, that   50
my affluence[1] over my niece is very small.—[*Aside to her*]
Turn round, Lydia, I blush for you!

SIR ANTHONY: May I not flatter myself that Miss Languish will assign what cause of dislike she can have to my son!—

[1] Influence.

Why don't you begin, Jack?—[*Aside to him*] Speak, you   55
puppy—speak!

MRS. MALAPROP: It is impossible, Sir Anthony, she can
have any.—She will not say she has.—[*Aside to her*] Answer,
hussy! why don't you answer?

SIR ANTHONY: Then, madam, I trust that a childish and   60
hasty predilection will be no bar to Jack's happiness.—
[*Aside to him*] Z—ds! sirrah! why don't you speak?

LYDIA [*aside*]: I think my lover seems as little inclined to
conversation as myself.—How strangely blind my aunt
must be!   65

ABSOLUTE: Hem! hem!—madam—hem!—[ABSOLUTE
attempts to speak, then returns to SIR ANTHONY]—Faith!
sir, I am so confounded!—and so—so—confused!—I told
you I should be so, sir,—I knew it.—The—the—tremor of
my passion entirely takes away my presence of mind.   70

SIR ANTHONY: But it don't take away your voice fool,
does it?—Go up, and speak to her directly!

   [ABSOLUTE *makes signs to* MRS. MALAPROP *to leave
   them together*]

MRS. MALAPROP: Sir Anthony, shall we leave them together?—[*Aside to her*] Ah! you stubborn, little
vixen!

SIR ANTHONY: Not yet, ma'am, not yet!—[*Aside to him*]   75
What the d—l are you at? unlock your jaws, sirrah, or——
                     [ABSOLUTE *draws near* LYDIA]

ABSOLUTE [*aside*]: Now heav'n send she may be too sullen
to look round!—I must disguise my voice.—[*Speaks in a
low hoarse tone*]——Will not Miss Languish lend an ear to
the mild accents of true love?—Will not——   80

SIR ANTHONY: What the d—l ails the fellow?—Why don't
you speak out?—not stand croaking like a frog in a
quinsy!—[1]

---

[1] Inflammation of the tonsils.

ABSOLUTE: The—the—excess of my awe, and my—my—
my modesty, quite choke me! 85

SIR ANTHONY: Ah! your *modesty* again!—I'll tell you what,
Jack, if you don't speak out directly, and glibly, too, I shall
be in such a rage!—Mrs. Malaprop, I wish the lady would
favour us with something more than a side-front!

[MRS. MALAPROP *seems to chide* LYDIA]

ABSOLUTE: So!—all will out I see! 90

[*Goes up to* LYDIA, *speaks softly*]

Be not surprised, my Lydia; suppress all surprise at
present.

LYDIA [*aside*]: Heav'ns! 'tis Beverley's voice!—Sure he
can't have imposed on Sir Anthony, too!—

[*Looks round by degrees, then starts up*]

Is this possible!—my Beverley!—how can this be?—my 95
Beverley?

ABSOLUTE [*aside*]: Ah! 'tis all over.

SIR ANTHONY: Beverley!—the devil!—Beverley!—What
can the girl mean?—This is my son, Jack Absolute!

MRS. MALAPROP: For shame, hussy! for shame!—your 100
head runs so on that fellow, that you have him always in
your eyes!—Beg Captain Absolute's pardon directly.

LYDIA: I see no Captain Absolute, but my loved Beverley!

SIR ANTHONY: Z—ds! the girl's mad!—her brain's turned
by reading! 105

MRS. MALAPROP: O' my conscience, I believe so!—What
do you mean by Beverley, hussy!—You saw Captain
Absolute before to-day; there he is—your husband that
shall be.

LYDIA: With all my soul, ma'am—when I refuse my 110
Beverley——

SIR ANTHONY: O! she's as mad as Bedlam![1]—or has this

---

[1] The hospital of St. Mary of Bethlehem, which was a lunatic asylum in the
eighteenth century. It was close to Moorfields, London.

fellow been playing us a rogue's trick!—Come here,
sirrah!—who the d—l are you?

ABSOLUTE: Faith, sir, I am not quite clear myself; but I'll   115
endeavour to recollect.

SIR ANTHONY: Are you my son, or not?—answer for your
mother, you dog, if you won't for me.

MRS. MALAPROP: Aye, sir, who are you? O mercy! I begin
to suspect!——   120

ABSOLUTE [*aside*]: Ye Powers of Impudence befriend me!—
[*Aloud*] Sir Anthony, most assuredly I am your wife's son;
and that I sincerely believe myself to be *yours* also, I hope
my duty has always shown.—Mrs. Malaprop, I am your
most respectful admirer—and shall be proud to add   125
affectionate nephew.—I need not tell my Lydia, that she
sees her faithful *Beverley*, who, knowing the singular generosity of her temper, assumed that name, and a station,
which has proved a test of the most disinterested love,
which he now hopes to enjoy in a more elevated character.   130

LYDIA [*sullenly*]: So!—there will be no elopement after all!

SIR ANTHONY: Upon my soul, Jack, thou art a very
impudent fellow![1] to do you justice, I think I never saw a
piece of more consummate assurance!

ABSOLUTE: O, you flatter me, sir—you compliment—'tis   135
my *modesty* you know, sir—my *modesty* that has stood in
my way.

SIR ANTHONY: Well, I am glad you are not the dull, insensible varlet you pretended to be, however!—I'm glad
you have made a fool of your father, you dog—I am.——   140
So this was your *penitence*, your *duty*, and *obedience!*—I
thought it was d—n'd sudden!—You *never heard their
names before*, not you!—*What!* The *Languishes* of Worcestershire, hey? —*if you could please me in the affair,* '*twas*

[1] Cf. Lord Foppington in Vanbrugh's *The Relapse*, IV. vi: 'Strike me dumb,
Tam, thou art a very impudent fellow.'

all you desired!—Ah! you dissembling villain!—What!— 145
[*pointing to* LYDIA] *she squints, don't she?*—*a little red-haired*
girl!—hey?—Why, you hypocritical young rascal—I
wonder you a'n't ashamed to hold up your head!

ABSOLUTE: 'Tis with difficulty, sir—I *am* confused—very
much confused, as you must perceive. 150

MRS. MALAPROP: O Lud! Sir Anthony!—a new light
breaks in upon me!—hey!—how! what! Captain, did *you*
write the letters then?—What!—am I to thank *you* for the
elegant compilation[1] of '*an old weather-beaten she-dragon*'
—hey?—O mercy! was it *you* that reflected on my parts 155
of speech?

ABSOLUTE: Dear sir! my modesty will be overpowered at
last, if you don't assist me.—I shall certainly not be able to
stand it!

SIR ANTHONY: Come, come, Mrs. Malaprop, we must for- 160
get and forgive—Odds life! matters have taken so clever[2]
a turn all of a sudden, that I could find in my heart, to be
so good-humoured! and so gallant!—hey! Mrs. Malaprop!

MRS. MALAPROP: Well, Sir Anthony, since *you* desire it,
we will not anticipate[3] the past;—so mind young people 165
—our retrospection[4] will now be all to the future.

SIR ANTHONY: Come, we must leave them together; Mrs.
Malaprop, they long to fly into each other's arms, I warrant! [*Aside*]—Jack—isn't the cheek as I said, hey?—and the
eye, you rogue!—and the lip—hey?—Come, Mrs. Mala- 170
prop, we'll not disturb their tenderness—theirs is the time
of life for happiness!——'*Youth's the season made for joy*'[5]
—[*Sings*]—hey!—Odds life! I'm in such spirits,—I don't

---

[1] Appellation.   [2] Neat.   [3] Exacerbate.

[4] Introspection. The line is laughable as it stands in that she says that they will
foresee the past and recall the future, a hope that has all the qualities of an Irish
'bull'.

[5] See p. 140.

know what I couldn't do!—Permit me, ma'am—[*Gives his hand to* MRS. MALAPROP] [*Sings*] Tol-de-rol!—'gad, I   175 should like a little fooling myself—Tol-de rol! de-rol!

   Exit singing, and handing MRS. MALAPROP [LYDIA *sits sullenly in her chair*]

ABSOLUTE [*aside*]: So much thought bodes me no good.— [*Aloud*] So grave, Lydia!

LYDIA: Sir!

ABSOLUTE [*aside*]: So!—egad! I thought as much!—That   180 d—n'd monosyllable has froze me!—[*Aloud*] What, Lydia, now that we are as happy in our friends' consent, as in our mutual vows——

LYDIA: [*peevishly*]. *Friends' consent*, indeed!

ABSOLUTE: Come, come, we must lay aside some of our   185 romance—a little *wealth* and *comfort* may be endured after all. And for your fortune, the lawyers shall make such settlements as——

LYDIA: *Lawyers!*—I *hate* lawyers!

ABSOLUTE: Nay then, we will not wait for their linger-   190 ing forms, but instantly procure the licence, and——

LYDIA: The *licence!*—I *hate* licence!

ABSOLUTE: O my love! be not so unkind!—thus let me en-treat——   [*Kneeling*]

LYDIA: Pshaw!—what signifies kneeling, when you know   195 I *must have* you?

ABSOLUTE [*rising*]: Nay, madam, there shall be no con-straint upon your inclinations, I promise you.—If I have lost your *heart*,—I resign the rest.—[*Aside*] 'Gad, I must try what a little *spirit* will do.   200

LYDIA [*rising*]: Then, sir, let me tell you, the interest you had there was acquired by a mean, unmanly imposition, and deserves the punishment of fraud.—What, you have been treating *me* like a *child!*—humouring my romance! and laughing, I suppose, at your success!   205

ABSOLUTE: You wrong me, Lydia, you wrong me.—Only
hear——

LYDIA: So, while *I* fondly imagined we were deceiving my
relations, and flattered myself that I should outwit and
incense them all—behold! my hopes are to be crushed at   210
once, by my aunt's consent and approbation—and *I* am
myself the only dupe at last! [*Walking about in heat*]—But
here, sir, here is the picture—*Beverley's* picture! [*taking a
miniature from her bosom*] which I have worn, night and
day, in spite of threats and entreaties!—There, sir [*flings*   215
it to him]—and be assured I throw the original from my
heart as easily.

ABSOLUTE: Nay, nay, ma'am, we will not differ as to that.
—Here [*taking out a picture*], here is Miss Lydia Languish.—
What a difference!—aye, *there* is the heav'nly assenting   220
smile that first gave soul and spirit to my hopes!—those
are the lips which sealed a vow, as yet scarce dry in Cupid's
calendar!—and there, the half resentful blush that *would*
have checked the ardour of my thanks.—Well, all that's
past!—all over indeed!—There, madam—in *beauty*, that   225
copy is not equal to you, but in my mind its merit over the
original, in being still the same, is such—that—I cannot
find in my heart to part with it.   [*Puts it up again*]

LYDIA [*softening*]: 'Tis *your own* doing, sir—I, I, I suppose you
are perfectly satisfied.   230

ABSOLUTE: O, most certainly—sure now this is much better
than being in love!—ha! ha! ha!—there's some spirit in
this!—What signifies breaking some scores of solemn
promises, all that's of no consequence, you know.—To be
sure people will say, that Miss didn't know her own mind   235
—but never mind that:—or perhaps they may be ill-
natured enough to hint, that the gentleman grew tired of
the lady and forsook her—but don't let that fret you.

LYDIA: There's no bearing his insolence.   [*Bursts into tears*]

Enter MRS. MALAPROP *and* SIR ANTHONY

MRS. MALAPROP [*Entering*]: Come, we must interrupt your   240
billing and cooing for a while.

LYDIA: This is worse than your treachery and deceit, you
base ingrate!   [*Sobbing*]

SIR ANTHONY: What the devil's the matter now!—Z—ds!
Mrs. Malaprop, this is the *oddest billing* and *cooing* I ever   245
heard!—but what the deuce is the meaning of it?—I'm
quite astonished!

ABSOLUTE: Ask the lady, sir.

MRS. MALAPROP: O mercy!—I'm quite analysed,[1] for my
part!—why, Lydia, what is the reason of this?   250

LYDIA: Ask the gentleman, ma'am.

SIR ANTHONY: Z—ds! I shall be in a frenzy!—why, Jack,
you are not come out to be any one else, are you?

MRS. MALAPROP: Aye, sir, there's no more trick, is there?
—you are not like Cerberus,[2] *three* gentlemen at once,   255
are you?

ABSOLUTE: You'll not let me speak—I say the lady can
account for this much better than I can.

LYDIA: Ma'am, you once commanded me never to think
of Beverley again—there is the man—I now obey you:—   260
for, from this moment, I renounce him for ever.

                                       Exit LYDIA

MRS. MALAPROP: O mercy! and miracles! what a turn here
is!—why sure, Captain, you haven't behaved disrespect-
fully to my niece?

SIR ANTHONY: Ha! ha! ha!—ha! ha! ha!—now I see it—   265
ha! ha! ha!—now I see it—you have been too lively,
Jack.

ABSOLUTE: Nay, sir, upon my word——

[1] Paralysed.
[2] Pluto's three-headed dog, who guarded the entrance to Hades.

SIR ANTHONY: Come, no lying, Jack—I'm sure 'twas so.

MRS. MALAPROP: O Lud! Sir Anthony!—O fie,   270
Captain!

ABSOLUTE: Upon my soul, ma'am——

SIR ANTHONY: Come, no excuses, Jack;—why, your father,
you rogue, was so before you:—the blood of the Absolutes
was always impatient.—Ha! ha! ha! poor little Lydia!—   275
why, you've frightened her, you dog, you have.

ABSOLUTE: By all that's good, sir—

SIR ANTHONY: Z—ds! say no more, I tell you.—Mrs.
Malaprop shall make your peace.—You must make his
peace, Mrs. Malaprop;—you must tell her 'tis Jack's way   280
—tell her 'tis all our ways—it runs in the blood of our
family!—Come, away, Jack—ha! ha! ha! Mrs. Malaprop
—a young villain!   [*Pushes him out*]

MRS. MALAPROP: O! Sir Anthony!—O fie, Captain!

Exeunt severally

Scene iii

The North Parade

Enter SIR LUCIUS O'TRIGGER

SIR LUCIUS: I wonder where this Cap. Absolute hides himself.—Upon my conscience!—these officers are always in
one's way in love affairs:—I remember I might have
married Lady Dorothy Carmine, if it had not been for a
little rogue of a major, who ran away with her before she   5
could get a sight of me!—And I wonder too what it is the
ladies can see in them to be so fond of them—unless it be
a touch of the old serpent[1] in 'em, that makes the little

[1] The tempter in the Garden of Eden: see Genesis iii.

creatures be caught, like vipers[1] with a bit of red cloth.[2]
—Hah!—isn't this the Captain coming?—faith it is!—   10
There is a probability of succeeding about that fellow,
that is mighty provoking!—Who the devil is he talking
to?   [*Steps aside*]

Enter CAPTAIN ABSOLUTE

ABSOLUTE: To what fine purpose I have been plotting! a
noble reward for all my schemes, upon my soul!—A little   15
gypsy![3]—I did not think her romance could have made
her so d—n'd absurd either—'Sdeath, I never was in a
worse humour in my life!—I could cut my own throat,
or any other person's, with the greatest pleasure in the
world!   20

SIR LUCIUS: O, faith! I'm in the luck of it—I never could
have found him in a sweeter temper for my purpose—to
be sure I'm just come in the nick! now to enter into conversation with him, and so quarrel genteelly.[4] [SIR LUCIUS
goes up to ABSOLUTE]——With regard to that matter,   25
Captain, I must beg leave to differ in opinion with you.

ABSOLUTE: Upon my word then, you must be a very subtle
disputant:—because, sir, I happened just then to be giving
no opinion at all.

SIR LUCIUS: That's no reason.—For give me leave to tell   30
you, a man may *think* an untruth as well as *speak* one.

ABSOLUTE: Very true, sir, but if a man never utters his
thoughts, I should think they might stand a chance of
escaping controversy.

SIR LUCIUS: Then, sir, you differ in opinion with me,   35
which amounts to the same thing.

---

[1] Vipers waste their venom on the cloth, and can then be picked up without
danger.
[2] The military uniform, 'redcoat'.
[3] Cheat.   [4] In a gentlemanly way.

ABSOLUTE: Hark'ee, Sir Lucius,—if I had not before known
you to be a gentleman, upon my soul, I should not have
discovered it at this interview:—for what you can drive at,
unless you mean to quarrel with me, I cannot conceive!   40

SIR LUCIUS: I humbly thank you, sir, for the quickness of
your apprehension [*Bowing*]—you have named the very
thing I would be at.

ABSOLUTE: Very well, sir—I shall certainly not baulk your
inclinations;—but I should be glad you would please to   45
explain your motives.

SIR LUCIUS: Pray, sir, be easy—the quarrel is a very pretty
quarrel as it stands—we should only spoil it, by trying to
explain it.—However, your memory is very short—or
you could not have forgot an affront you passed on me   50
within this week.—So no more, but name your time and
place.

ABSOLUTE: Well, sir, since you are so bent on it, the sooner
the better;—let it be this evening—here, by the Spring-
Gardens.[1]—We shall scarcely be interrupted.   55

SIR LUCIUS: Faith! that same interruption in affairs of this
nature, shows very great ill-breeding.—I don't know
what's the reason, but in England, if a thing of this kind
gets wind, people make such a pother,[2] that a gentleman
can never fight in peace and quietness.—However, if it's   60
the same to you, Captain, I should take it as a particular
kindness, if you'd let us meet in King's-Mead-Fields,[3] as a
little business will call me there about six o'clock, and I
may dispatch both matters at once.

ABSOLUTE: 'Tis the same to me exactly.—A little after six,   65
then, we will discuss this matter more seriously.

[1] A summer rendezvous for public breakfasts, teas, concerts, and fireworks. It
lay on the Bathwick side of the Pulteney Bridge.
[2] Commotion.
[3] Sheridan himself had lived in Kingsmead Street. Open fields lay beyond it.

SIR LUCIUS: If you please, sir, there will be very pretty small-sword[1] light, tho' it won't do for a long shot.—So that matter's settled! and my mind's at ease!

Exit SIR LUCIUS

Enter FAULKLAND, *meeting* ABSOLUTE

ABSOLUTE: Well met.—I was going to look for you.—O,   70
Faulkland! all the dæmons of spite and disappointment have conspired against me! I'm so vexed, that if I had not the prospect of a resource in being knocked o' the head by and by, I should scarce have spirits to tell you the cause.   75

FAULKLAND: What can you mean?—Has Lydia changed her mind?—I should have thought her duty and inclination would now have pointed to the same object.

ABSOLUTE: Aye, just as the eyes do of a person who squints: —when her love-eye was fixed on me—t'other—her eye   80
of duty, was finely obliqued:—but when duty bid her point that the same way—off t'other turned on a swivel, and secured its retreat with a frown!

FAULKLAND: But what's the resource you——

ABSOLUTE: O, to wind up the whole, a good-natured Irish-   85
man here has—[*mimicking* SIR LUCIUS]—begged leave to have the pleasure of cutting my throat—and I mean to indulge him—that's all.

FAULKLAND: Prithee, be serious.

ABSOLUTE: 'Tis fact, upon my soul.—Sir Lucius O'Trigger   90
—you know him by sight—for some affront, which I am sure I never intended, has obliged me to meet him this evening at six o'clock:—'tis on that account I wished to see you—you must go with me.

FAULKLAND: Nay, there must be some mistake, sure.—Sir   95

---

[1] A light sword or rapier for thrusting only.

Lucius shall explain himself—and I dare say matters may
be accommodated:—but this evening did you say?—I
wish it had been any other time.

ABSOLUTE: Why?—there will be light enough:—there will
(as Sir Lucius says) 'be very pretty small-sword light, 100
though it won't do for a long shot.'—Confound his long
shots!

FAULKLAND: But I am myself a good deal ruffled, by a
difference I have had with Julia—my vile tormenting
temper has made me treat her so cruelly, that I shall not 105
be myself till we are reconciled.

ABSOLUTE: By heav'ns, Faulkland, you don't deserve her.

Enter SERVANT, *gives* FAULKLAND *a letter*

FAULKLAND: O Jack! this is from Julia.—I dread to open
it.—I fear it may be to take a last leave—perhaps to bid
me return her letters—and restore——O! how I suffer 110
for my folly!

ABSOLUTE: Here—let me see. [*Takes the letter and opens it*]
Aye, a final sentence indeed!—'tis all over with you,
faith!

FAULKLAND: Nay, Jack—don't keep me in suspense. 115

ABSOLUTE: Hear then.—'*As I am convinced that my dear*
FAULKLAND'*s own reflections have already upbraided him for
his last unkindness to me, I will not add a word on the subject.—
I wish to speak with you as soon as possible.—Yours ever and
truly,* JULIA.'—There's stubbornness and resentment for 120
you! [*Gives him the letter*] Why, man, you don't seem one
whit the happier at this.

FAULKLAND: O, yes, I am—but—but——

ABSOLUTE: Confound your *buts*.—You never hear anything
that would make another man bless himself, but you 125
immediately d—n it with a *but*.

FAULKLAND: Now, Jack, as you are my friend, own
honestly—don't you think there is something forward—
something indelicate in this haste to forgive?—Women
should never sue for reconciliation:—that should always   130
come from us.—They should retain their coldness till
wooed to kindness—and their *pardon*, like their *love*,
should 'not unsought be won.'[1]

ABSOLUTE: I have not patience to listen to you:—thou'rt
incorrigible!—so say no more on the subject.—I must go   135
to settle a few matters—let me see you before six—
remember—at my lodgings.—A poor industrious devil
like me, who have toiled, and drudged, and plotted to gain
my ends, and am at last disappointed by other people's
folly—may in pity be allowed to swear and grumble a   140
little;—but a captious sceptic in love,—a slave to fretfulness and whim—who has no difficulties but of his own
creating—is a subject more fit for ridicule than com-
passion!   *Exit* ABSOLUTE

FAULKLAND: I feel his reproaches!—yet I would not change   145
this too exquisite nicety for the gross content with which
he tramples on the thorns of love.—His engaging me in
this duel, has started an idea in my head, which I will
instantly pursue.—I'll use it as the touchstone[2] of Julia's
sincerity and disinterestedness—if her love prove pure and   150
sterling[3] ore—my name will rest on it with honour!—and
once I've stamped it there, I lay aside my doubts for ever:
—but if the dross of selfishness, the allay[4] of pride pre-
dominate—'twill be best to leave her as a toy for some less
cautious fool to sigh for.   *Exit* FAULKLAND   155

[1] From *Paradise Lost*, viii. 502-3:
> Her virtue, and the conscience of her worth,
> That would be wooed, and not unsought be won.

[2] A black stone used to test the purity of gold or silver, but the word is also used
of any criterion.

[3] Of true worth.   [4] Alloy.

Act V scene i

JULIA: How this message has alarmed me! What dreadful
accident can he mean? why such charge to be alone?—O
Faulkland!—how many unhappy moments!—how many
tears have you cost me!

Enter FAULKLAND

JULIA: What means this?—why this caution, Faulkland?   5
FAULKLAND: Alas! Julia, I am come to take a long
farewell.
JULIA: Heav'ns! what do you mean?
FAULKLAND: You see before you a wretch, whose life is
forfeited.—Nay, start not!—the infirmity of my temper
has drawn all this misery on me.—I left you fretful and   10
passionate—an untoward accident drew me into a
quarrel—the event is, that I must fly this kingdom
instantly.—O Julia, had I been so fortunate as to have
called you mine entirely, before this mischance had
fallen on me, I should not so deeply dread my banish-   15
ment!—
JULIA: My soul is oppressed with sorrow at the nature of
your misfortune: had these adverse circumstances arisen
from a less fatal cause, I should have felt strong comfort in
the thought that I could now chase from your bosom   20

every doubt of the warm sincerity of my love.—My heart has long known no other guardian—I now entrust my person to your honour—we will fly together.—When safe from pursuit, my father's will may be fulfilled—and I receive a legal claim to be the partner of your sorrows, 25 and tenderest comforter. Then on the bosom of your wedded Julia, you may lull your keen regret to slumbering; while virtuous love, with a cherub's hand, shall smooth the brow of upbraiding thought, and pluck the thorn from compunction. 30

FAULKLAND: O Julia! I am bankrupt in gratitude! but the time is so pressing, it calls on you for so hasty a resolution. Would you not wish some hours to weigh the advantages you forego, and what little compensation poor Faulkland can make you beside his solitary love? 35

JULIA: I ask not a moment.—No, Faulkland, I have loved you for yourself: and if I now, more than ever, prize the solemn engagement which so long has pledged us to each other, it is because it leaves no room for hard aspersions on my fame, and puts the seal of duty to an act of love.— 40 —But let us not linger—Perhaps this delay——

FAULKLAND: 'Twill be better I should not venture out again till dark.—Yet am I grieved to think what numberless distresses will press heavy on your gentle disposition!

JULIA: Perhaps your fortune may be forfeited by this 45 unhappy act.—I know not whether 'tis so—but sure that alone can never make us unhappy.—The little I have will be sufficient to support us; and exile never should be splendid.

FAULKLAND: Aye, but in such an abject state of life, my 50 wounded pride perhaps may increase the natural fretfulness of my temper, till I become a rude, morose companion, beyond your patience to endure. Perhaps the recollection of a deed my conscience cannot justify, may haunt

me in such gloomy and unsocial fits, that I shall hate the 55
tenderness that would relieve me, break from your arms,
and quarrel with your fondness!

JULIA: If your thoughts should assume so unhappy a bent,
you will the more want some mild and affectionate spirit
to watch over and console you:—one who, by bearing 60
your infirmities with gentleness and resignation, may
teach you *so* to bear the evils of your fortune.

FAULKLAND: Julia, I have proved you to the quick! and
with this useless device I throw away all my doubts. How
shall I plead to be forgiven this last unworthy effect of my 65
restless, unsatisfied disposition?

JULIA: Has no such disaster happened as you related?

FAULKLAND: I am ashamed to own that it was all pretended;
yet in pity, Julia, do not kill me with resenting a fault
which never can be repeated: but sealing, this once, my 70
pardon, let me to-morrow, in the face of heaven, receive
my future guide and monitress, and expiate my past folly,
by years of tender adoration.

JULIA: Hold, Faulkland!—that you are free from a crime
which I before feared to name, heaven knows how sin- 75
cerely I rejoice!—These are tears of thankfulness for that!
But that your cruel doubts should have urged you to an
imposition that has wrung my heart, gives me now a pang,
more keen than I can express!

FAULKLAND: By heav'ns! Julia—— 80

JULIA: Yet hear me.—My father loved you, Faulkland! and
you preserved the life that tender parent gave me; in his
presence I pledged my hand—joyfully pledged it—where
before I had given my heart. When, soon after, I lost that
parent, it seemed to me that Providence had, in Faulkland, 85
shown me whither to transfer, without a pause, my grateful duty, as well as my affection: hence I have been content
to bear from you what pride and delicacy would have

forbid[1] me from another.—I will not upbraid you, by
repeating how you have trifled with my sincerity.—— 90

FAULKLAND: I confess it all! yet hear——

JULIA: After such a year of trial[2]—I might have flattered
myself that I should not have been insulted with a new
probation of my sincerity, as cruel as unnecessary! I now
see it is not in your nature to be content, or confident 95
in love. With this conviction—I never will be yours.
While I had hopes that my persevering attention, and un-
reproaching kindness might in time reform your temper,
I should have been happy to have gained a dearer influence
over you; but I will not furnish you with a licensed power 100
to keep alive an incorrigible fault, at the expense of one
who never would contend with you.

FAULKLAND: Nay, but Julia, by my soul and honour, if after
this——

JULIA: But one word more.—As my faith has once been 105
given to you, I never will barter it with another.—I shall
pray for your happiness with the truest sincerity; and the
dearest blessing I can ask of heaven to send you, will be to
charm you from that unhappy temper, which alone has
prevented the performance of our solemn engagement.— 110
All I request of *you* is, that you will yourself reflect upon
this infirmity, and when you number up the many true
delights it has deprived you of—let it not be your *least*
regret, that it lost you the love of one—who would have
followed you in beggary through the world! 115

FAULKLAND: She's gone!—for ever!—There was an awful
resolution in her manner, that riveted me to my place.—
O fool!—dolt!—barbarian!—Curst as I am, with more
imperfections than my fellow-wretches, kind Fortune
sent a heaven-gifted cherub to my aid, and, like a ruffian, 120
I have driven her from my side!—I must now haste to my

---

[1] Forbidden.   [2] Trial.

appointment.—Well my mind is tuned for such a scene.—
I shall wish only to become a principal in it, and reverse the
tale my cursed folly put me upon forging here.—O love!
—tormentor!—fiend! whose influence, like the moon's, 125
acting on men of dull souls, makes idiots of them, but
meeting subtler spirits, betrays their course, and urges
sensibility to madness![1]   *Exit*

Enter MAID *and* LYDIA

MAID: My mistress, ma'am, I know, was here just now—
perhaps she is only in the next room.   *Exit* MAID 130
LYDIA: Heigh-ho!—Though he has used me so, this fellow
runs strangely in my head. I believe one lecture from my
grave cousin will make me recall him.

Enter JULIA

LYDIA: O Julia, I am come to you with such an appetite for
consolation.—Lud! Child, what's the matter with you? 135
—You have been crying!—I'll be hanged, if that Faulkland has not been tormenting you!
JULIA: You mistake the cause of my uneasiness!—Something *has* flurried me a little.—Nothing that you can
guess at.—[*Aside*] I would not accuse Faulkland to a sister! 140
LYDIA: Ah! whatever vexations you may have, I can assure
you mine surpass them.—You know who Beverley proves
to be?
JULIA: I will now own to you, Lydia, that Mr. Faulkland
had before informed me of the whole affair. Had young 145
Absolute been the person you took him for, I should not

---

[1] 'Lunatic' is derived from the Latin 'luna', the moon. The idea is similar to that
in *Midsummer Night's Dream*, V. i:
> The lunatic, the lover, and the poet,
> Are of imagination all compact.

have accepted your confidence on the subject, without a
serious endeavour to counteract your caprice.

LYDIA: So, then, I see I have been deceived by everyone!—
but I don't care—I'll never have him.　　　　　　　　　　150

JULIA: Nay, Lydia——

LYDIA: Why, is it not provoking? when I thought we were
coming to the prettiest distress imaginable, to find myself
made a mere Smithfield bargain[1] of at last.—There had
I projected one of the most sentimental elopements!—so　155
becoming a disguise!—so amiable a ladder of ropes!—
Conscious[2] moon—four horses—Scotch parson[3]—with
such surprise to Mrs. Malaprop—and such paragraphs in
the newspapers!—O, I shall die with disappointment!

JULIA: I don't wonder at it!　　　　　　　　　　　　　　160

LYDIA: Now—sad reverse!—what have I to expect, but,
after a deal of flimsy[4] preparation, with a bishop's licence,[5]
and my aunt's blessing, to go simpering up to the altar; or
perhaps be cried three times in a country-church, and have
an unmannerly fat clerk ask the consent of every butcher　165
in the parish to join John Absolute and Lydia Languish,
spinster! O, that I should live to hear myself called
spinster!

JULIA: Melancholy, indeed!

LYDIA: How mortifying, to remember the dear delicious　170
shifts I used to be put to, to gain half a minute's conversation with this fellow!—How often have I stole forth, in
the coldest night in January, and found him in the garden,

[1] A marriage of interest in which money is the main consideration (*N.E.D.*).
Smithfield was a London cattle-market.

[2] Sympathetic, a meaning close to the Latin origin of the word.

[3] Since minors could not be married in England without the consent of parents
or guardians, impetuous couples eloped to Scotland where they merely had to
signify their wish to marry before two witnesses.

[4] Paltry.

[5] Permission to marry in the church of a parish in which one of the parties
resides. The alternative method—marriage by banns—is then described by Lydia.

stuck like a dripping statue!—There would he kneel to me
in the snow, and sneeze, and cough so pathetically! he   175
shivering with cold, and I with apprehension! and while
the freezing blast numbed our joints, how warmly would
he press me to pity his flame, and glow with mutual ardour!—Ah, Julia, that was something like being in
love.   180

JULIA: If I were in spirits, Lydia, I should chide you only by
laughing heartily at you: but it suits more the situation of
my mind, at present, earnestly to entreat you, not to let a
man, who loves you with sincerity, suffer that unhappiness
from your caprice, which I know too well caprice can in- 185
flict.

LYDIA: O Lud![1] what has brought my aunt here?

Enter MRS. MALAPROP, FAG, *and* DAVID

MRS. MALAPROP: So! so! here's fine work!—here's fine
suicide, paracide,[2] and simulation[3] going on in the fields!
and Sir Anthony not to be found to prevent the anti-   190
strophe![4]

JULIA: For heaven's sake, madam, what's the meaning of
this?

MRS. MALAPROP: That gentleman can tell you—'twas he
enveloped[5] the affair to me.   195

LYDIA [*to* FAG]: Do, sir, will you, inform us.

FAG: Ma'am, I should hold myself very deficient in every
requisite that forms the man of breeding, if I delayed a
moment to give all the information in my power to a
lady so deeply interested in the affair as you are.   200

LYDIA: But quick! quick, sir!

FAG: True, ma'am, as you say, one should be quick in

[1] A corruption of 'Lord!'
[2] Parricide, the murder of one's father or near relation.
[3] Dissimulation.   [4] Catastrophe.   [5] Developed.

divulging matters of this nature; for should we be tedious, perhaps while we are flourishing[1] on the subject, two or three lives may be lost!   205

LYDIA: O patience!—Do, ma'am, for heaven's sake! tell us what is the matter!

MRS. MALAPROP: Why, murder's the matter! slaughter's the matter! killing's the matter!—but he can tell you the perpendiculars.[2]   210

LYDIA: Then, prithee, sir, be brief.

FAG: Why then, ma'am—as to murder—I cannot take upon me to say—and as to slaughter, or man-slaughter, that will be as the jury finds it.

LYDIA: But who, sir—who are engaged in this?   215

FAG: Faith, ma'am, one is a young gentleman whom I should be very sorry anything was to happen to—a very pretty behaved gentleman!—We have lived much together, and always on terms.

LYDIA: But who is this? who! who! who!   220

FAG: My master, ma'am—my master—I speak of my master.

LYDIA: Heavens! What, Captain Absolute!

MRS. MALAPROP: O, to be sure, you are frightened now!

JULIA: But who are with him, sir?

FAG: As to the rest, ma'am, this gentleman can inform you   225
better than I.

JULIA [to DAVID]: Do speak, friend.

DAVID: Look'ee, my lady—by the Mass! there's mischief going on.—Folks don't use to meet for amusement with fire-arms, fire-locks, fire-engines, fire-screens, fire-office,[3]   230
and the devil knows what other crackers beside!—This, my lady, I say, has an angry favour.[4]

---

[1] Speaking in a flowery way.   [2] Particulars.

[3] David is so alarmed that he reels off the names of everything connected with 'fire' rather than with 'fire-arms'. The 'fire-office' was the office of an insurance company dealing with fires.

[4] Inflamed look, as of a wound.

JULIA: But who is there beside Captain Absolute, friend?

DAVID: My poor master—under favour, for mentioning 235 him first.—You know me, my lady—I am David—and my master of course is, or *was*, Squire Acres.—Then comes Squire Faulkland.

JULIA: Do, ma'am, let us instantly endeavour to prevent mischief.   240

MRS. MALAPROP: O fie—it would be very inelegant in us: —we should only participate[1] things.

DAVID: Ah! do, Mrs. Aunt, save a few lives.—They are desperately given, believe me.—Above all, there is that bloodthirsty Philistine,[2] Sir Lucius O'Trigger.   245

MRS. MALAPROP: Sir Lucius O'Trigger!—O mercy! have they drawn poor little dear Sir Lucius into the scrape?— why, how you stand, girl! you have no more feeling than one of the Derbyshire putrefactions![3]

LYDIA: What are we to do, madam?   250

MRS. MALAPROP: Why, fly with the utmost felicity[4] to be sure, to prevent mischief—here, friend—you can show us the place?

FAG: If you please, ma'am, I will conduct you.—David, do you look for Sir Anthony.   *Exit* DAVID 255

MRS. MALAPROP: Come, girls!—this gentleman will exhort[5] us.—Come, sir, you're our envoy[6]—lead the way, and we'll precede.[7]

FAG: Not a step before the ladies for the world!

---

[1] Precipitate.   [2] A harassing enemy.

[3] Petrifactions. The 'wonders of the Peak' were often described, and R. Brookes's *General Gazetteer* (10th ed., 1797) says of Pool's Hole, near Buxton, that it 'contains many stalactitious concretions, and several curious representations both of art and nature, produced by the petrifying water continually dropping from the rock'.

[4] Velocity.   [5] Escort.
[6] Convoy.   [7] Proceed.

MRS. MALAPROP: You're sure you know the spot?   260
FAG: I think I can find it, ma'am; and one good thing is we shall hear the report of the pistols as we draw near, so we can't well miss them: never fear, ma'am, never fear.

Exit, he talking

Scene ii

South Parade

Enter ABSOLUTE, *putting his sword under his great-coat*

ABSOLUTE: A sword seen in the streets of Bath[1] would raise as great an alarm as a mad-dog. How provoking this is in Faulkland!—never punctual! I shall be obliged to go without him at last.—O, the devil! here's Sir Anthony! ——how shall I escape him?   5

[*Muffles up his face, and takes a circle to go off*]

Enter SIR ANTHONY

SIR ANTHONY: How one may be deceived at a little distance! Only that I see he don't know me, I could have sworn that was Jack!—Hey!—'Gad's life; it is.—Why, Jack—what are you afraid of?—hey!—sure I'm right.— Why, Jack—Jack Absolute!   [*Goes up to him*]   10
ABSOLUTE: Really, sir, you have the advantage of me:—I don't remember ever to have had the honour——my name is Saunderson, at your service.
SIR ANTHONY: Sir, I beg your pardon—I took you—hey! —hey!—Why, z—ds! it is——Stay—— [*Looks up to his*   15 *face*] So, so—your humble servant, Mr. Saunderson!—

---

[1] Beau Nash had had both parties arrested whenever he had heard of a challenge to a duel at Bath.

Why, you scoundrel, what tricks are you after
now?

ABSOLUTE: O! a joke, sir, a joke!—I came here on purpose
to look for you, sir.   20

SIR ANTHONY: You did! well, I am glad you were so lucky:
—but what are you muffled up so for?—what's this for?—
hey?

ABSOLUTE: 'Tis cool, sir; isn't it?—rather chilly somehow:
—but I shall be late—I have a particular engagement.   25

SIR ANTHONY: Stay.—Why, I thought you were looking
for me?—Pray, Jack, where is't you are going?

ABSOLUTE: Going, sir!

SIR ANTHONY: Aye—where are you going?

ABSOLUTE: Where am I going?   30

SIR ANTHONY: You unmannerly puppy!

ABSOLUTE: I was going, sir, to—to—to—to Lydia—sir, to
Lydia—to make matters up if I could;—and I was looking
for you, sir, to—to——

SIR ANTHONY: To go with you, I suppose.—Well, come   35
along!

ABSOLUTE: O! z—ds! no, sir, not for the world!—I wished
to meet with you, sir,—to—to—to——You find it cool,
I'm sure, sir—you'd better not stay out.

SIR ANTHONY: Cool!—not at all.—Well, Jack—and what   40
will you say to Lydia?

ABSOLUTE: O, sir, beg her pardon, humour her—promise
and vow:—but I detain you, sir—consider the cold air on
your gout.

SIR ANTHONY: O, not at all!—not at all!—I'm in no hurry.   45
—Ah! Jack, you youngsters, when once you are wounded
here—[*Putting his hand to* ABSOLUTE'S *breast*] Hey! what
the deuce have you got here?

ABSOLUTE: Nothing, sir—nothing.

SIR ANTHONY: What's this?—here's something d—d hard!   50

ABSOLUTE: O, trinkets, sir! trinkets—a bauble for Lydia!

SIR ANTHONY: Nay, let me see your taste. [*Pulls his coat
open, the sword falls*] Trinkets!—a bauble for Lydia!—
z—ds! sirrah, you are not going to cut her throat, are
you?   55

ABSOLUTE: Ha! ha! ha!—I thought it would divert you, sir
tho' I didn't mean to tell you till afterwards.

SIR ANTHONY: You didn't?—Yes, this is a very diverting
trinket, truly!

ABSOLUTE: Sir, I'll explain to you.—You know, sir, Lydia   60
is romantic—dev'lish romantic, and very absurd of course:
—now, sir, I intend, if she refuses to forgive me—to un-
sheathe this sword—and swear—I'll fall upon its point, and
expire at her feet!

SIR ANTHONY: Fall upon a fiddle-stick's end!—why, I   65
suppose it is the very thing that would please her.—Get
along, you fool.—

ABSOLUTE: Well, sir, you shall hear of my success—you
shall hear.—'O Lydia!—forgive me, or this pointed steel'
—says I.   70

SIR ANTHONY: 'O, booby! stab away and welcome'—says
she.—Get along! —and d—n your trinkets!

Exit ABSOLUTE

Enter DAVID *running*

DAVID: Stop him! stop him! Murder! thief! fire!—Stop
fire! Stop fire!—O! Sir Anthony—call! call! bid 'm
stop! Murder! Fire!   75

SIR ANTHONY: Fire! murder! where?

DAVID: Oons! he's out of sight! and I'm out of breath for
my part! O, Sir Anthony, why didn't you stop him? why
didn't you stop him?

SIR ANTHONY: Z—ds! the fellow's mad!—Stop whom?   80
stop Jack?

DAVID: Aye, the Captain, Sir!—there's murder and slaughter.——

SIR ANTHONY: Murder!

DAVID: Aye, please you, Sir Anthony, there's all kinds of 85 murder, all sorts of slaughter to be seen in the fields: there's fighting going on, sir—bloody sword-and-gun fighting!

SIR ANTHONY: Who are going to fight, dunce?

DAVID: Everybody that I know of, Sir Anthony:—every- 90 body is going to fight, my poor master, Sir Lucius O'Trigger, your son, the Captain——

SIR ANTHONY: O, the dog!—I see his tricks.—Do you know the place?

DAVID: King's-Mead-Fields. 95

SIR ANTHONY: You know the way?

DAVID: Not an inch;—but I'll call the mayor—aldermen— constables—church-wardens—and beadles[1]—we can't be too many to part them.

SIR ANTHONY: Come along—give me your shoulder![2] 100 we'll get assistance as we go.—The lying villain!—Well, I shall be in such a frenzy—So—this was the history of his trinkets! I'll bauble him!   *Exeunt*

Scene iii

King's-Mead-Fields

SIR LUCIUS *and* ACRES, *with pistols*

ACRES: By my valour! then, Sir Lucius, forty yards is a good distance.—Odds levels and aims!—I say it is a good distance.

---

[1] A parish official relieving the poor and keeping order in church.
[2] Let me lean on you. Sir Anthony has the gout.

SIR LUCIUS: Is it for muskets or small field-pieces?[1] upon
my conscience, Mr. Acres, you must leave those things to
me.—Stay now—I'll show you.—[*Measures paces along the
stage*] There now, that is a very pretty distance—a pretty
gentleman's distance.

ACRES: Z—ds! we might as well fight in a sentry-box!—I
tell you, Sir Lucius, the farther he is off, the cooler I shall
take my aim.

SIR LUCIUS: Faith! then I suppose you would aim at him
best of all if he was out of sight!

ACRES: No, Sir Lucius—but I should think forty, or eight
and thirty yards——

SIR LUCIUS: Pho! pho! nonsense! Three or four feet
between the mouths of your pistols is as good as a mile.

ACRES: Odds bullets, no!—by my valour! there is no merit
in killing him so near:—do, my dear Sir Lucius, let me
bring him down at a long shot:—a long shot, Sir Lucius,
if you love me!

SIR LUCIUS: Well—the gentleman's friend and I must settle
that.—But tell me now, Mr. Acres, in case of an accident,
is there any little will or commission I could execute for
you!

ACRES: I am much obliged to you, Sir Lucius—but I don't
understand——

SIR LUCIUS: Why, you may think there's no being shot at
without a little risk—and if an unlucky bullet should carry
a quietus[2] with it—I say it will be no time then to be
bothering you about family matters.

ACRES: A quietus!

SIR LUCIUS: For instance now—if that should be the case—

---

[1] Movable artillery.

[2] 'Quietus est' meant, in medieval Latin, 'he is quit (of his incumbrances)'.
Here, the sense is of a final discharge from life, as in Hamlet's 'When he himself
might his quietus make/With a bare bodkin' (III. i).

would you choose to be pickled and sent home?—or
would it be the same to you to lie here in the Abbey?[1]—   35
I'm told there is very snug lying in the Abbey.

ACRES: Pickled!—Snug lying in the Abbey!—Odds
tremors! Sir Lucius, don't talk so!

SIR LUCIUS: I suppose, Mr. Acres, you never were
engaged in an affair of this kind before?   40

ACRES: No, Sir Lucius, never before.

SIR LUCIUS: Ah! that's a pity!—there's nothing like being
used to a thing.—Pray now, how would you receive the
gentleman's shot?

ACRES: Odds files![2]—I've practised that—there, Sir Lucius   45
—there [*Puts himself in an attitude*]——a side-front, hey?—
Odd! I'll make myself small enough:—I'll stand edgeways.

SIR LUCIUS: Now—you're quite out—for if you stand so
when I take my aim——   [*Levelling at him*]   50

ACRES: Z—ds! Sir Lucius—are you sure it is not cocked?

SIR LUCIUS: Never fear.

ACRES: But—but—you don't know—it may go off of its
own head![3]

SIR LUCIUS: Pho! be easy.—Well, now if I hit you in the   55
body, my bullet has a double chance—for if it misses a
vital part on your right side—'twill be very hard if it don't
succeed on the left!

ACRES: A vital part!

SIR LUCIUS: But, there—fix yourself so.—[*Placing him*]   60
Let him see the broad-side of your full front—there—now
a ball or two may pass clean thro' your body, and never
do any harm at all.

ACRES: Clean thro' me!—a ball or two clean thro' me!

---

[1] Beneath the floor of the Abbey Church at Bath. At this time it was nearly
paved with memorial slabs.
[2] A file was a sword without edges used in fencing.
[3] Accord.

SIR LUCIUS: Aye—may they—and it is much the genteelest   65
attitude into the bargain.

ACRES: Look'ee! Sir Lucius—I'd just as lieve[1] be shot in an
awkward posture as a genteel one—so, by my valour! I
will stand edge-ways.

SIR LUCIUS [*Looking at his watch*]: Sure they don't mean to   70
disappoint us.—Hah!—no, faith—I think I see them
coming.

ACRES: Hey!—what!—coming!——

SIR LUCIUS: Aye.—Who are those yonder getting over the
stile?   75

ACRES: There are two of them indeed!—well—let them
come—hey, Sir Lucius! we—we—we—we—won't run.—

SIR LUCIUS: Run!

ACRES: No—I say—we *won't* run, by my valour!

SIR LUCIUS: What the devil's the matter with you?   80

ACRES: Nothing—nothing—my dear friend—my dear
Sir Lucius—but—I—I—I don't feel quite so bold, somehow—as I did.

SIR LUCIUS: O fie!—consider your honour.

ACRES: Aye—true—my honour—Do, Sir Lucius, edge in a   85
word or two every now and then about my honour.

SIR LUCIUS [*looking*]: Well, here they're coming.

ACRES: Sir Lucius—if I wa'n't with you, I should almost
think I was afraid—if my valour should leave me!—Valour
will come and go.   90

SIR LUCIUS: Then, pray, keep it fast, while you have it.

ACRES: Sir Lucius—I doubt[2] it is going—yes—my valour
is certainly going!—it is sneaking off!—I feel it oozing
out as it were at the palms of my hands!

SIR LUCIUS: Your honour—your honour.—Here they are.   95

ACRES: O mercy!—now—that I were safe at *Clod-Hall* or
could be shot before I was aware!

---

[1] More usually 'lief': gladly.   [2] Fear.

Enter FAULKLAND *and* ABSOLUTE

SIR LUCIUS: Gentlemen, your most obedient—hah!—what
   Captain Absolute!—So, I suppose, sir, you are come here,
   just like myself—to do a kind office, first for your friend—   100
   then to proceed to business on your own account.

ACRES: What, Jack!—my dear Jack!—my dear friend!

ABSOLUTE: Hark'ee, Bob, *Beverley's* at hand.

SIR LUCIUS: Well Mr. Acres—I don't blame your saluting
   the gentleman civilly.—So, Mr. Beverley, [*to* FAULK-   105
   LAND], if you'll choose your weapons, the Captain and I
   will measure the ground.

FAULKLAND: *My* weapons, sir!

ACRES: Odds life! Sir Lucius, I'm not going to fight Mr.
   Faulkland; these are my particular friends.   110

SIR LUCIUS: What, sir, did not you come here to fight Mr.
   Acres?

FAULKLAND: Not I, upon my word, sir.

SIR LUCIUS: Well, now, that's mighty provoking! But I
   hope, Mr. Faulkland, as there are three of us come on   115
   purpose for the game—you won't be so cantankerous as
   to spoil the party by sitting out.

ABSOLUTE: O pray, Faulkland, fight to oblige Sir Lucius.

FAULKLAND: Nay, if Mr. Acres is so bent on the matter——

ACRES: No, no, Mr. Faulkland—I'll bear my disappoint-   120
   ment like a Christian.—Look'ee, Sir Lucius, there's no
   occasion at all for me to fight; and if it is the same to you,
   I'd as lieve let it alone.

SIR LUCIUS: Observe me, Mr. Acres—I must not be trifled
   with. You have certainly challenged somebody—and you   125
   came here to fight him.— Now, if that gentleman is willing to represent him—I can't see, for my soul, why it
   isn't just the same thing.

ACRES: Why no, Sir Lucius—I tell you, 'tis one Beverley

I've challenged—a fellow, you see, that dare not show his   130
face! If *he* were here, I'd make him give up his pretensions
directly!—

ABSOLUTE: Hold, Bob—let me set you right—there is no
such man as *Beverley* in the case.—The person who assumed that name is before you; and as his pretensions are   135
the same in both characters, he is ready to support them in
whatever way you please.

SIR LUCIUS: Well, this is lucky!—Now you have an
opportunity——

ACRES: What, quarrel with my dear friend Jack Absolute—   140
not if he were fifty Beverleys! Z—ds! Sir Lucius, you
would not have me be so unnatural.

SIR LUCIUS: Upon my conscience, Mr. Acres, your valour
has *oozed* away with a vengeance!

ACRES: Not in the least! Odds backs[1] and abettors! I'll be   145
your second with all my heart—and if you should get a
quietus, you may command me entirely. I'll get you a
snug lying in the *Abbey here*; or *pickle* you, and send you
over to Blunderbuss-Hall, or anything of the kind with
the greatest pleasure.   150

SIR LUCIUS: Pho! pho! you are little better than a coward.

ACRES: Mind, gentlemen, he calls me a *coward*; coward was
the word, by my valour!

SIR LUCIUS: Well, sir?

ACRES: Look'ee, Sir Lucius, 'tisn't that I mind the word   155
coward—*coward* may be said in joke. But if you had called
me a *poltroon*,[2] odds daggers and balls!——

SIR LUCIUS: Well, sir?

ACRES:——I should have thought you a very ill-bred
man.

---

[1] Supporters. Cf. Congreve's *The Old Bachelor*, II. 1: 'Ah my Hector of Troy,
welcome my bully, my back.'

[2] Completely without spirit or courage.

SIR LUCIUS: Pho! you are beneath my notice.   160

ABSOLUTE: Nay, Sir Lucius, you can't have a better second than my friend Acres.—He is a most *determined dog*— called in the country, *Fighting Bob*.—He generally *kills a man a week*; don't you, Bob?

ACRES: Aye—at home!   165

SIR LUCIUS: Well then, Captain, 'tis we must begin— so come out, my little counsellor[1] [*draws his sword*], and ask the gentleman, whether he will resign the lady, without forcing you to proceed against him.

ABSOLUTE: Come on then, sir; [*draws*] since you won't   170 let it be an amicable suit, here's *my reply*.

Enter SIR ANTHONY, DAVID, *and the* WOMEN

DAVID: Knock 'em all down, sweet Sir Anthony, knock down my master in particular—and bind his hands over to their good behaviour!

SIR ANTHONY: Put up, Jack, put up, or I shall be in a   175 frenzy.—How came you in a duel sir?

ABSOLUTE: Faith, sir, that gentleman can tell you better than I; 'twas he called on me, and you know, sir, I serve his Majesty.[2]

SIR ANTHONY: Here's a pretty fellow! I catch him going to   180 cut a man's throat, and he tells me, he serves his Majesty! —Zounds! sirrah, then how durst you draw the King's sword against one of his subjects?

ABSOLUTE: Sir, I tell you! That gentleman called me out, without explaining his reasons.   185

SIR ANTHONY: Gad! sir, how came you to call my son out, without explaining your reasons?

---

[1] In its Irish sense of 'barrister'. This is a contemptuous reference to Acres as one fond of disputation rather than fighting.

[2] An army officer could not refuse a challenge.

SIR LUCIUS: Your son, sir, insulted me in a manner which my honour[1] could not brook.

SIR ANTHONY: Zounds! Jack, how durst you insult the gentleman in a manner which his honour could not brook? 190

MRS. MALAPROP: Come, come, let's have no honour before ladies—Captain Absolute, come here—How could you intimidate us so?—Here's Lydia has been terrified to death 195 for you.

ABSOLUTE: For fear I should be killed, or escape, ma'am?

MRS. MALAPROP: Nay, no delusions[2] to the past—Lydia is convinced;—speak child.

SIR LUCIUS: With your leave, ma'am, I must put in a word 200 here—I believe I could interpret the young lady's silence —Now mark——

LYDIA: What is it you mean, sir?

SIR LUCIUS: Come, come, Delia, we must be serious now— this is no time for trifling. 205

LYDIA: 'Tis true, sir; and your reproof bids me offer this gentleman my hand, and solicit the return of his affections.

ABSOLUTE: O! my little angel, say you so?—Sir Lucius—I perceive there must be some mistake here.—With regard to the affront which you affirm I have given you—I can 210 only say, that it could not have been intentional.—And as you must be convinced, that I should not fear to support a real injury—you shall now see that I am not ashamed to atone for an inadvertency.—I ask your pardon.—But for this lady, while honoured with her approbation, I will 215 support my claim against any man whatever.

SIR ANTHONY: Well said, Jack and I'll stand by you, my boy.

ACRES: Mind, I give up all my claim—I make no pretensions to anything in the world—and if I can't get a wife without fighting for her, by my valour! I'll live a bachelor. 220

---

[1] Fighting to satisfy one's sense of honour.   [2] Allusions.

SIR LUCIUS: Captain, give my your hand—an affront hand-
somely acknowledged becomes an obligation—and as for
the lady—if she chooses to deny her own handwriting
here——   [*Takes out letters*]

MRS. MALAPROP: O, he will dissolve[1] my mystery!—Sir   225
Lucius, perhaps there's some mistake—perhaps, I can
illuminate——

SIR LUCIUS: Pray, old gentlewoman, don't interfere where
you have no business.—Miss Languish, are you my Delia,
or not?   230

LYDIA: Indeed, Sir Lucius, I am not.
                    [LYDIA *and* ABSOLUTE *walk aside*]

MRS. MALAPROP: Sir Lucius O'Trigger—ungrateful as you
are—I own the soft impeachment[2]—pardon my blushes,
I am Delia.

SIR LUCIUS: You Delia!—pho! pho! be easy.[3]   235

MRS. MALAPROP: Why, thou barbarous Vandyke[4]—those
letters are mine.—When you are more sensible of my
benignity—perhaps I may be brought to encourage your
addresses.

SIR LUCIUS: Mrs. Malaprop, I am extremely sensible of   240
your condescension;[5] and whether you or Lucy have put
this trick upon me, I am equally beholden to you.—And
to show you I'm not ungrateful, Captain Absolute! since
you have taken that lady from me, I'll give you my Delia
into the bargain.   245

ABSOLUTE: I am much obliged to you, Sir Lucius; but
here's our friend, Fighting Bob, unprovided for.

SIR LUCIUS: Hah! little Valour—here, will you make your
fortune?

---

[1] Solve.   [2] Gentle reproach.

[3] Don't be sought after. The word is still used in this sense on the Stock Exchange.

[4] Vandal: the tribe of barbarians that plundered Rome in the fifth century.

[5] Kindliness towards an inferior, but used here ironically.

ACRES: Odds wrinkles! No.—But give me your hand, Sir   250
Lucius; forget and forgive; but if ever I give you a
chance of *pickling* me again, say Bob Acres is a dunce,
that's all.

SIR ANTHONY: Come, Mrs. Malaprop, don't be cast down
—you are in your bloom yet.   255

MRS. MALAPROP: O Sir Anthony!—men are all barbarians——   [*All retire but* JULIA *and* FAULKLAND]

JULIA [*aside*]: He seems dejected and unhappy—not sullen.
—There was some foundation, however, for the tale he
told me.—O woman! how true should be your judgment,   260
when your resolution is so weak!

FAULKLAND: Julia—how can I sue for what I so little
deserve? I dare not presume—yet Hope is the child of
Penitence.

JULIA: Oh! Faulkland, you have not been more faulty in   265
your unkind treatment of me, than I am now in wanting
inclination to resent it. As my heart honestly bids me
place my weakness to the account of love, I should be
ungenerous not to admit the same plea for yours.

FAULKLAND: Now I shall be blest indeed!   270

[SIR ANTHONY *comes forward*]

SIR ANTHONY: What's going on here?—So you have been
quarrelling too, I warrant.—Come, Julia, I never inter-
fered before; but let me have a hand in the matter at last.—
All the faults I have ever seen in my friend Faulkland,
seemed to proceed from what he calls the *delicacy* and   275
warmth of his affection for you.—There, marry him
directly, Julia, you'll find he'll mend surprisingly!

[*The rest come forward*]

SIR LUCIUS: Come now, I hope there is no dissatisfied
person, but what is content: for as I have been disappointed myself, it will be very hard if I have not the   280
satisfaction of seeing other people succeed better——

ACRES: You are right, Sir Lucius.—So, Jack, I wish you joy—Mr. Faulkland the same.—Ladies,—come now, to show you I'm neither vexed nor angry, odds tabors and pipes! I'll order the fiddles in half an hour, to the New 285 Rooms[1]—and I insist on your all meeting me there.

SIR ANTHONY: Gad! sir, I like your spirit; and at night we single[2] lads will drink a health to the young couples, and a husband to Mrs. Malaprop.

FAULKLAND: Our partners are stolen from us, Jack—I hope 290 to be congratulated by each other—*yours* for having checked in time, the errors of an ill-directed imagination, which might have betrayed an innocent heart; and *mine*, for having, by her gentleness and candour, reformed the unhappy temper of one who by it made wretched whom he 295 loved most, and tortured the heart he ought to have adored.

ABSOLUTE: Well, Jack, we have both tasted the bitters, as well as the sweets, of love—with this difference only, that *you* always prepared the bitter cup for yourself, while *I*——

LYDIA: Was always obliged to *me* for it, hey! Mr. Modesty? 300 ——But come, no more of that—our happiness is now as unallayed as general.

JULIA: Then let us study to preserve it so; and while Hope pictures to us a flattering scene of future bliss, let us deny its pencil those colours which are too bright to be lasting. 305 —When hearts deserving happiness would unite their fortunes, Virtue would crown them with an unfading garland of modest, hurtless flowers; but ill-judging Passion will force the gaudier rose into the wreath, whose thorn offends them, when its leaves are dropped![3] *Exeunt omnes* 310

---

[1] See p. 88, n. 6.

[2] Sir Anthony is a widower. The first edition of the play contains the line, 'Sir Anthony, your wife, Lady Absolute, was fond of books' (II. i). Although Sheridan eliminated this from the third edition, I don't think he intended IV. ii. 118, to suggest that Jack Absolute was an illegitimate child.

[3] The speech ends with two lines of blank verse.

EPILOGUE

By the Author

Spoken by Mrs. Bulkley

Ladies for *you*—I heard our poet say—
He'd try to coax some *moral* from his play:
'One moral's plain'—cried I—'without more fuss;
Man's social happiness all rests on us—
Thro' all the drama—whether damned[1] or not—   5
Love gilds the *scene*, and *women* guide the *plot*.
From ev'ry rank—obedience is our due—
D'ye doubt?—The world's great stage shall prove it true.'

The cit[2]—well skilled to shun domestic strife—
Will sup abroad;—but first—he'll ask his *wife:*   10
John Trot,[3] his friend—for once, will do the same,
But then—he'll just *step home to tell my dame.*—

The *surly squire*—at noon resolves to rule,
And half the day—zounds! madam is a fool!
Convinced at night—the vanquished victor[4] says,   15
'Ah! Kate! *you women have such coaxing ways!*'—

---

[1] Unsuccessful at its first performance, and therefore not acted again.
[2] Citizen, but more particularly middle-class merchants and tradespeople.
[3] Commonly used in the eighteenth century for an ill-bred man.
[4] From Dryden's 'Alexander's Feast', l. 97:

> At length with love and wine at once opprest
> The vanquish'd victor sunk upon her breast.

The *jolly toper* chides each tardy blade,[1]—
Till reeling Bacchus calls on Love for aid:
Then with each toast, he sees fair bumpers swim,
And kisses Chloe[2] on the sparkling brim!   20

Nay, I have heard that statesmen—great and wise—
Will *sometimes* counsel with a lady's eyes;
The servile suitors—watch her various face,
She smiles preferment—or she frowns disgrace,
Curtsies a pension here—there nods a place.   25

Nor with less awe, in scenes of humbler life,
Is *viewed* the *mistress*, or is *heard* the *wife*.
The poorest peasant of the poorest soil,
The child of poverty and heir to toil—
Early from radiant Love's impartial light,   30
Steals one small spark, to cheer his world of night:
Dear spark!—that oft thro' winter's chilling woes,
Is all the warmth his little cottage knows!
The wand'ring *tar*—who not for *years* has press'd
The widowed partner of his *day* of rest—   35
On the cold deck—far from her arms removed—
Still hums the ditty which his Susan[3] loved:
And while around the cadence rude is blown,
The boatswain whistles in a softer tone.

[1] Of corn, especially malting barley.

[2] Another name frequently to be found in the love poetry of the previous hundred years, and particularly in that of Matthew Prior.

[3] The ditty is John Gay's ballad, 'Sweet William's Farewell to Black eyed Susan'. Stanza six runs:

> If to far India's coast we sail
>   Thy eyes are seen in di'monds bright
>   Thy breath is Africk's spicy gale,
>   Thy skin is ivory, so white.
> Thus ev'ry beauteous object that I view,
> Wakes in my soul some charm of lovely Sue.

The *soldier*, fairly[1] proud of wounds and toil,   40
Pants for the *triumph* of his Nancy's[2] smile;
But ere the battle, should he list' her cries,
The lover trembles—and the hero dies!
That heart, by war and honour steeled to fear,
Droops on a sigh, and sickens at a tear!   45

But ye more cautious—ye nice judging few,
Who give to beauty only beauty's due,
Tho' friends to Love—*ye* view with deep regret
Our conquests marred—and triumphs incomplete,
'Till polished wit more lasting charms disclose,   50
And judgment fix the darts which beauty throws!
—In female breasts did sense and merit rule,
The lover's mind would ask no other school;
Shamed into sense—the scholars of our eyes,
Our beaux[3] from *gallantry*[4] would soon be wise;   55
Would glady light, their homage to improve,
The lamp of Knowledge at the torch of Love!

[1] Justly.

[2] The conventional name for a soldier's girl. It is the name of the heroine of another play Sheridan was associated with —*The Camp*.

[3] Fine gentlemen who dance attendance on women.

[4] Playing with the sense of intrigue in love as contrasted with bravery on the field of battle.

NOTES

1. LYDIA LANGUISH'S BOOKS (pp. 33–34 and 39)

The more obscure titles were identified by G. H. Nettleton in the *Jl. of Eng. and Germ. Phil.*, V (Oct. 1905), 4, and in *The Major Dramas of . . . Sheridan* (Boston, 1906), pp. lxviii–lxxvii. Many of them were sentimental novels of little real worth. *The Town and Country Magazine* (Dec., 1773). p. 669, reviewed *The Fatal Connexion* in one phrase only, 'Fresh materials for the trunk makers'; and *The London Magazine* (Sept., 1773) said it was 'romantic nonsense, as usual'. The better-known works include famous novels by Smollett (1721–71), Sterne (1713–68), and Mackenzie (1745–1831), as well as more prurient material by Ovid and Scarron (1610–60). Highly serious books by Hester Chapone (1727–1801), Chesterfield (1694–1773), and James Fordyce (1720–96), completed the list.

l.4: *The Reward of Constancy*. Possibly *The Happy Pair or, Virtue and Constancy Rewarded* (1771).

l.6: *The Fatal Connexion. A Novel*. By Mrs. Fogerty. 2 vols. (1773).

l.8: *The Mistakes of the Heart, or, Memoirs of Lady Caroline Pelham and Lady Victoria Nevil. In a Series of Letters. Published by M. Treyssac de Vergy*. . . . . Printed for J. Murdoch. 3 vols. (1769).

l.11: *The Delicate Distress and The Gordian Knot. By the Authors of Henry and Frances* (1769–70). The first was by Elizabeth Griffith (d. 1793), and the second by her husband Richard Griffith (d. 1788).

l.13: *The Memoirs of Lady Woodford* (1771).

l.25: *The Adventures of Peregrine Pickle* includes *The Memoirs of a Lady of Quality*. By Tobias Smollett (1751; 5th ed., 1773).

l.25: *The Tears of Sensibility. Translated from the French of M. D'Arnaud* [Baculard D'Arnaud (1718–1805)] *by J. Murdoch*. 2 vols. (1773).

l.26: *The Expedition of Humphry Clinker*. By Tobias Smollett (1771).

l.28: *A Sentimental Journey through France and Italy*. By Laurence Sterne. 2 vols. (1768).

l.30: *The Whole Duty of Man* (1659). This devotional work was usually published in octavo or duodecimo, but since Lucy refers to 'the great one', it is possible that she was alluding to the *Works of the learned and pious Author of The Whole Duty of Man*, published in folio in 1704 and 1723.

l.168: *The Adventures of Roderick Random*. By Tobias Smollett (1748).

l.168: *The Innocent Adultery. Translated from the French*. By S[amuel] C[roxall] (1722). This was Paul Scarron's *L'Adultère Innocente*, but R. C. Rhodes has argued (in *The Plays and Poems of . . . Sheridan*, 1928, i. 12) that the reference is likely to be to something more recently published and suggested *Harriet, or The Innocent Adultress* (1771).

l.169: *The History of Lord Aimsworth, and the Honourable Charles Hartford, Esq., in a Series of Letters*. By the author of *Dorinda Catsby*, and *Ermina, or the Fair Recluse*. 3 vols. (1773).

l.170: Publius Ovidius Naso (43 B.C.–A.D. 17); the most recent translations of his works were: *The Art of Love* (1757); *Epistles, with his Amours* (1761); *Metamorphoses* (trans. N. Bailey, 1759).

l.171: *The Man of Feeling*. By Henry Mackenzie (1771).

l.171: *Letters on the Improvement of the Mind. Addressed to a Young Lady* (1773). By Mrs. Chapone.

l.172: *Sermons to Young Women* (1765; 7th ed., 1771). By James Fordyce.

l.176: *Letters written by the late Right Honourable Philip Dormer Stanhope, Earl of Chesterfield, to his Son, Philip Stanhope, Esq.*, 2 vols. (1774).

2. MRS. MALAPROP'S 'NICE DERANGEMENT OF EPITAPHS'

Mrs. Malaprop is anxious to show what a fine vocabulary she possesses, and hopes to be admired as something of a bluestocking or 'progeny of learning'. Consequently she displays her superior powers in the high-sounding: some of the words resemble what she is groping to express, others are nowhere near it. In this she is not unlike Win Jenkins, the servant in Smollett's *Humphry Clinker* who learns up her mistress's phrases but brings them out again in such ridiculous misuses as 'the whole family have been in such a constipation'. We laugh with Win because she is a good-hearted, if scatterbrained, soul, but we laugh at Mrs. Malaprop because of her ludicrous vanity.

It is customary to say that Sheridan took this trait from Mrs. Tryfor't in his mother's comedy, *A Journey to Bath*. She is described thus: ''Tis the vainest poor creature, and the fondest of hard words, which without miscalling, she always takes care to misapply.' This is very close to Julia's description of Mrs. Malaprop's 'select words, so ingeniously *misapplied, without being mispronounced*.' Some of the literary puns (like 'antistrophe' for 'catastrophe', or 'allegory' for 'alligator') seem strained when we read them, but delight an audience because of the air of superiority with which she pronounces them. The contrast between her vanity and her howlers is rich in humour.

Many of them are rather mechanical puns, but the more ordinary they are the more she preens herself, and the more the audience enjoys her self-satisfaction. Sometimes her transitions produce an Irish 'bull', as in the extraordinary play on 'retrospection' in IV, ii. 166. Sometimes she blunders into good sense and pleases us with the neat phrase 'soft impeachment' (V. iii. 233). Other words surprise and interest us: 'the pineapple of politeness' tickles our fancy. 'You forfeit my malevolence' has a curious irony, whether that is intended by Sheridan or not. So, too, has 'my oracular tongue'.

Altogether, Mrs. Malaprop's use of language gives her a certain bumptious vitality, but her assertiveness justly draws upon her Sir Lucius's reproof—'Be easy!'

3. THE SONGS

p. 53, n. 6: 'When absent from my soul's delight'

> When absent from my soul's delight,
> What terrors fill my troubled breast,
> Once more return'd to thy loved sight,
> Hope too returns, my fears have rest.
>
> If the light breezes curl the wave,
> Move but a leaf or bend a flow'r,
> Fears for your safety never leave
> This heart, the victim of your pow'r.
>
> In love there's no long happiness,
> Its pains are far superior found:
> A hope of joy we scarce possess
> But 'tis in some new sorrow drowned.
>
> (from *Twelve Songs set to Music by William Jackson of Exeter. Opera Quarta*. London. Printed for the Author, and Sold at the Music Shops. n.d. Song VI, pp. 14–19)

p. 54, n. 1: 'Go, gentle gales!'

> Go, gentle gales, go gentle gales
> And bear my sighs away
> To Delia's ear, to Delia's ear,
> The tender notes convey.
>
> As some sad turtle his lost love deplores
> And with deep murmurs fills the sounding shores,
> Thus far from Delia to the wood I mourn,
> Alike unheard, unpitied, and forlorn.
>
> Go gentle gales, go gentle gales
> And bear my sighs away.
> Come Delia come, Come Delia come,
> Ah why this long delay?

Ye flow'rs that droop forsaken by the spring,
Ye birds that left by summer cease to sing,
Ye trees that fade when autumn heats remove,
Say, is not absence death to those that love!

> (from the same set of songs as above. Song V,
> pp. 10–15)

p. 54, n. 2: 'My heart's my own.'

My heart's my own, my will is free,
And so shall be my voice;
No mortal man shall wed with me,
Till first he's made my choice.

Let parent's rule, cry nature's laws;
And children still obey;
And is there then no saving clause
Against tyrannic sway.

> (from Act I of Isaac Bickerstaff's *Love in a Village*,
> 1762)

p. 101, n. 5: 'Youth's the season made for joy.'

Youth's the season made for joys,
   Love is then our duty;
She alone who that employs,
   Well deserves her beauty.
     Let's be gay,
     While we may,
Beauty's a flower, despised in decay.

Let us drink and sport today,
   Ours is not tomorrow.
Love with youth flies swift away,
   Age is nought but sorrow.
     Dance and sing,
     Time's on the wing,
Life never knows the return of spring.

> (from Act II. Sc. IV of Gay's *The Beggar's Opera*,
> 1728)

DATE			